REPRESENTATION

Written especially for undergraduate students, *Representation* synthesizes and updates our understandings of representation – and the tools for its analysis – for use in the new mediascape.

Jenny Kidd uses an engaging range of current examples and a lively style to explore a number of key questions reflecting existing and contemporary debates about representation.

These key questions include: Who 'owns' and manages representations? Whose realities are foregrounded, and whose are consigned to invisibility? To what extent are increased opportunities for self-representation altering the landscape? And what happens to representation within the noisy, playful and often subversive communications of the Internet?

Kidd considers the political, social and cultural importance of representation across a broad spectrum of cultural and creative industries.

This examination of the relationship between media/cultural representations and the construction of reality, identity and society makes it an ideal text for students that need to get to grips with this core thematic of media and cultural studies.

Jenny Kidd is Lecturer in the School of Journalism, Media and Cultural Studies, Cardiff University. Her research interests include digital media, museums and participation. She is the author of *Museums in the New Mediascape* (2014) and co-editor of *Challenging History in the Museum* (2014) and *Performing Heritage* (2011).

KEY IDEAS IN MEDIA & CULTURAL STUDIES

The *Key Ideas in Media and Cultural Studies* series covers the main concepts, issues, debates and controversies in contemporary media and cultural studies. Titles in the series constitute authoritative, original essays rather than literary surveys, but are also written explicitly to support undergraduate teaching. The series provides students and teachers with lively and original treatments of key topics in the field.

REPRESENTATION

Jenny Kidd

Routledge
Taylor & Francis Group

LONDON AND NEW YORK

First published 2016
by Routledge
2 Park Square, Milton Park, Abingdon, Oxon OX14 4RN

and by Routledge
711 Third Avenue, New York, NY 10017

Routledge is an imprint of the Taylor & Francis Group, an informa business

British Library Cataloguing in Publication Data
A catalogue record for this book is available from the British Library

Library of Congress Cataloging in Publication Data
Kidd, Jenny.
Representation / by Jenny Kidd.
pages cm. -- (Key ideas in media and cultural studies)
Includes bibliographical references and index.
1. Mass media. 2. Imagery (Psychology) 3. Semiotics. I. Title.
P91.K375 2015
302.23--dc23
2015020133

ISBN: 978-1-138-01669-9 (hbk)
ISBN: 978-1-138-02071-9 (pbk)
ISBN: 978-1-315-66678-5 (ebk)

Typeset in Times New Roman
by Taylor & Francis Books
Printed in Great Britain by Ashford Colour Press Ltd, Gosport, Hants

MIX
Paper from
responsible sources
FSC
www.fsc.org FSC® C011748

CONTENTS

FIGURES

ACKNOWLEDGEMENT

Having studied media representations in a variety of contexts for more than 13 years I have relished the opportunity in this book to consolidate my thinking in this area, and to synthesize existing theory with emergent discourses, particularly around digital media and self-representation.

Thanks are due to the editorial team at Routledge, particularly Natalie Foster, Sheni Kruger and the reviewers of the initial book proposal. I also thank Fiona Kidd for her input on the drafts of the opening chapters.

All of the chapters in this book have evolved from lectures on the 'Representations' module I run for all first year undergraduates in the School of Journalism, Media and Cultural Studies at Cardiff University. It is a module I enjoy teaching immensely, not least because I get to work with a crack team of Teaching Assistants who have included Hugh Griffiths, Xin Zhang, Dafina Paca, Susana Sampaio Dias, Judith Fathallah, James Rendell and Hiu Chan. In our meetings around lectures, we delight in sharing the responses of students to the subject matter, how we challenge them, and how every year they challenge us with the range of media they consume, the multitude of ways they interact with it, and the questions they wish to explore. This book is for those students.

INTRODUCTION
THE ONGOING SIGNIFICANCE OF REPRESENTATION

I write this opening on the day following the 70th Anniversary of the Liberation of Auschwitz, and the attendant revelations about the towering horrors concealed within that camp. Yesterday our media – not least the news and social networks – were awash with grainy still and moving images from that day 70 years ago, and the clear and considered voices of the survivors filtered over the radio. Many of those survivors had travelled to Auschwitz for a high profile memorial event attended by dignitaries from around the world. The anniversary had been the subject of intense international interest, and underpinned by the realization that for the next decennial, there may be few, if any, survivors left to tell their stories. This last point raises some significant questions with regard to the continued representation of those events, and of those whose lives – and life narratives – were forever impacted by their experiences within that camp, and indeed the many other camps: Who will continue to speak for the survivors (if anyone)? What presentations of their stories will be seen as appropriate in future years? Who will regulate their use and re-use, especially in our converged media ecology? Are there avenues for their use – and perhaps exploitation – that are yet to be fully explored? Will a limited number of images and narratives become the accepted 'truth' of the prisoner experience by the time we reach the centenary, or bi-centenary? And crucially, what will be the relationship between representation and remembering (even forgetting) over time? Jen Webb and others have questioned whether the Holocaust remains 'unrepresentable'; its horror being 'so vast that it cannot be reduced and contained by representation' (Webb 2009: 4, but see also Steyn 2014). They remind us of Theodor Adorno's assertion in 1951 that 'To write poetry after Auschwitz is barbaric' (Adorno 1967). Christopher Prendergast links this perspective with post-modernism, and with the associated undermining of scholarly enquiry into representations more broadly but states that 'this claim is entirely false. Everything is representable' (2000: 1). He goes on to say: 'It is not that representation as such is impossible; it is rather that it fails in its task' (2000: 2). The difference is an important one. Prendergast here alludes to the constructive nature of representation; and its limitations. Such a subject is of course an emotive one, but it brings home very powerfully the responsibility to think ethically about representations and their real world consequences. We begin to see that representations are ensnared in complex and infinite entanglements with identity, consumption, production and the regulation of culture, and of our media; that they are caught up in what has been called the 'circuit of culture' (Hall 1997). Representation is, Stuart Hall argues, 'one of the central practices which produce culture' (Hall 1997: 1) and its influence is thus hard to overstate.

Representation remains one of the core thematics of media and cultural studies and its understanding is a key component of media scholarship at both undergraduate and postgraduate level. The study of representations provides a sound basis and a range of methodologies for analysing texts, rendering them penetrable, and surprising, fields of study. This book synthesizes and updates our understandings of representation – and the tools for its analysis – for use in our new mediascape. This is a challenge that is undoubtedly overdue given the range of ways in which media, and their points of access, have diversified in recent years. It explores how audiences have traditionally been positioned in relation to meaning; asks questions about whose realities remain foregrounded and whose are silenced (or indeed, remain silent); explores who 'owns' and manages representations and whether this is changing; investigates what happens when differing representations collide; and how (indeed whether) increased opportunities for self-representation are challenging the landscape. Provocatively perhaps, it also asks readers to consider whether media studies' pre-occupation with representation might in itself be bad for representation.

The study of representation has historically been deemed important in the study of communications because of the limited range of available resources we have to produce representations of the world, of people, events and places. It is understood that the way we do this is never neutral. When people create representations of the world there are agendas at play, and particular sets of ideas, values, attitudes and identities assumed and normalized. There are thus issues of power, ownership, authenticity, and meaning at stake; nothing less than what comes to be seen as common sense, and is accepted about the world. In the opening paragraphs of this introduction, I explored the extent of those ramifications; for the representation of Holocaust narratives, we are not only concerned with how the past is seen and interpreted in the present, but with the real world political, social, cultural, ethical and moral consequences of those interpretations.

This book is about all of that. It sits between the study of our media and cultural industries and their audiences, looking instead at content; its implications and how it can be read. It sees the media and culture as an ensemble of texts and representations that can be unpacked. It is a book about getting to grips with how these might be analyzed and understood; about why it is important that we ask questions about the representations we are 'given' by the creators of cultural products. What is of interest here is how meaning is constructed as, and becomes, common sense in the media and cultural industries; through representation. Through soap operas, news reports, films, exhibitions, music, magazines, art and books our understandings of the world – and of people – are, in part at least, forged. This book will explore how representations, rather than simply presenting or mirroring reality, actually help to re-present it, or even create it anew. How the various 'languages' of our media produce 'meaning'. In this light, the mirror on the front of this book becomes a provocation; the relationship between representation and reality is a central recurrent tension.

THE BUILDING BLOCKS OF MEANING

The study of representation concerns itself with the construction of meaning. At its most basic level, meaning is constructed through language, signs and symbols, but these processes are never value free. The decisions we make about which word-signs, images and forms our representations take matter; those decisions being infused with intent, ideology and bias.

To continue our pre-occupation with history to illustrate this, let's take for a moment the red poppy as a symbol of remembrance. If we remind ourselves that, as Stuart Hall says, 'Things "in themselves" rarely if ever have any one, single, fixed and unchanging meaning' (Hall 1997: 3) we can begin to explore just how, and in what ways, this symbolism has taken hold. We might note that the poppy displayed in differing contexts varies in connotations (in a copy of a gardening magazine, or in a painting, perhaps), but how successfully and thoroughly, especially on a lapel during the month of November, the association with remembrance is made (certainly within the UK, New Zealand and Australian contexts). This is so much the case that the phenomenon has become the subject of academic scrutiny investigating how this symbol has come to signify with such intensity and even at times ferocity (Iles 2008). Nicholas Saunders introduces this enquiry as follows: 'Tragic yet uplifting, lethal but comforting, the story of the Remembrance Poppy is international in spirit yet intimately personal.' He goes on to note however that it is 'volatile' (Saunders 2002: 2–3).

The poppy recalls the battlefields of World War I, still and silent after the carnage of war, where the corn poppy grew amongst the trenches, simple and ephemeral. Red; evocative of blood spilt, intensity of emotion, and stark warnings. *In Flanders Fields*, written in 1915 by Canadian war poet John McCrae, canonized that connection with the immortal words: 'If ye break faith with us who die / We shall not sleep, though poppies grow/ In Flanders fields.' The poppy became a continued shorthand for the sacrifices of war, aided in the UK by its ongoing association with the Royal British Legion, for whom it has become not only a logo, but a registered trademark. For many in the UK, the red poppy and the 'poppy appeal' (as it is known) have become synonymous, but what we are noting here is that there is nothing natural or inevitable about that connection, it is a work of construction; 'representation cannot be confined to an original, real or authentic link between a thing and what stands for it' (Hartley et al. 2012: 154). Objects – things – people – are open to interpretation. We bring our own sets of experiences, emotions and identity constructs with us to our interpretations of them. A red poppy means something particular to me because I am a British person in the twenty-first century. If I were in Ancient Greece, it *might* recall for me the story of Morpheus, the God of Dreams. In Urdu writings it is seen as a symbol of martyrdom and love. In China it is an unwelcome reminder of the opium wars, as UK Prime Minister David Cameron discovered when he wore one on his lapel during a visit in 2010 (White 2010).

Meaning is thus not stable. A red poppy does not *mean* anything, meaning is what we attribute to it. It is us that give it a name, and give it a value (cultural, financial, historical, even organizational in the case of the Royal British Legion). Meaning is dependent on culture, geography, language, heritage, education, and it is through processes of representation that it is inscribed; through the 'words we use ... the stories we tell ... the images ... we produce, [and] the emotions we associate' (Hall 1997: 3). As is already becoming apparent, our representations, and individuals' interpretations of them, do not inevitably possess trans-cultural validity.

There is a coda to this exploration of the poppy in the form of the 2014 commemorative activities around the centenary of the outbreak of World War I and, in particular, the installation of Paul Cummins and Tom Piper's evolving work *Blood Swept Lands and Seas of Red* in the moat of the Tower of London (Figure 0.1). As an aside, it is worth readers reflecting on what is lost in the reproduction of the image overleaf in black and white;

Figure 0.1 Blood Swept Lands and Seas of Red installation at the Tower of
London, 2014. Image: author's own

in what ways is the work's power diminished in this particular
representation?

The staggering popularity of *Blood Swept Lands and Seas of
Red* was a reminder of what a potent symbol the poppy continues
to be within the United Kingdom; an accessible and familiar way
into remembrance. Mark Brown in *The Guardian* reflected that the
piece was 'the most visited and talked about public art installation
for a generation' and cites an estimate of more than 5 million
visitors in four months (Brown 2014). Each of the 888,246 poppies
in the Tower's moat represented one British life lost in World War I.
Many who visited had a direct connection with the war dead, or
indeed with those who continue to serve in places of conflict, and
used the installation as a conduit for telling their own stories via
social and other media. In time, others shared via these routes

pictures of their purchased poppies as they began to arrive in the post; for like the poppies in Flanders fields, the poppies at the Tower were ephemeral too.

Blood Swept Lands and Seas of Red raised many questions with respect to representation, and which were debated hotly in the many column inches given over to it in the press. Why were British dead being commemorated and not the many more fatalities throughout Europe? Was being an audience for the project merely a visual experience or social spectacle rather than an intellectual engagement? Where were the white poppies; the symbols of peace? Was this simply an exercise in Nationalism? What were the limitations of the piece's capacity to represent? Was the installation changing forever the patterns and performances of remembrance within and beyond the UK? This last question reminds us of the constructive nature of representations, as Jen Webb notes, 'the processes of representation do not simply make connections, relationships and identities *visible*: they actually *make* those connections, relationships and identities' (Webb 2009: 10). The artwork had catalyzed a renewed enthusiasm for remembrance – and a new way of enacting it as individuals, institutions and as publics – which may or may not be lasting. Given the questions raised, the work was seen by some to be a highly problematic representation to have as a lynchpin in the UK's commemorative activities. Jonathan Jones (also in *The Guardian*) wrote possibly the most scathing critique of the piece, calling it a 'deeply aestheticised, prettified and toothless war memorial' and even 'a lie' (Jones 2014), More meaningful, he argued, would be a moat 'filled with barbed wire and bones' (ibid.).

But we might ask whether such a representation would have filled the gulf in understanding Jones identifies. Would it have done more than evoke, provoke and emote? Would it have been any less of a deceit? Comprehension is perhaps an unrealistic goal of such representations, demanding far more than they can – or should – be expected to give, not least in the name of art. As Gill Branston and Roy Stafford note, 'No representation can "contain" more than a fraction of its real-world subject' (2010: 129). We will see this in evidence time and again in the chapters that follow.

THE POLITICS OF REPRESENTATION

So why, then, is the study of representation important? Why does all of this matter to those who are interested in the media, communications, culture? Because it is only through thinking about how and where our image of the world is forged that we can begin to understand it. Because to this day many groups, communities and individuals consider themselves to be vastly *under*-represented, on screen for example. Because to this day many groups, communities and individuals consider themselves to be dangerously *mis*-represented, in ethnographic exhibitions for example. Because stereotypes can be funny, but they can also be limiting, crass, persistent and poisonous. We may have come a long way from the hypodermic syringe model of media effects, but the media and culture we consume do still have a bearing on how we view the world. They impact upon how we might view those who live in other world contexts, or who we might not encounter in our everyday lives. In analyzing these building blocks of meaning and asking questions about why particular kinds of representations are offered up to us over others, we can better understand why our images of the world are skewed in the ways they inevitably are.

I contend that it is important that we remain focused on representation even in the light of accusations that its study might be outdated, self-indulgent or lacking in impact. We should wish to be creative practitioners who are politically engaged, astute, ethical, and enlightened as to the 'real world' consequences of the decisions we make in the production and circulation of cultural texts. This means taking stock of how, not least since Stuart Hall's original study of *Representations* (1997), the mediascape continues to shift. Branston and Stafford suggest in the *Media Student's Book* that the term representation is also a nod to the capacity much media have to 're-present, over and over again, certain images, stories, situations'. In so doing they 'seem "natural" or familiar – and thereby marginalize, or even exclude other images, making those *un*familiar or even threatening' (2010: 106). So, for example, if we only see images of disabled people as marginalized, or as victims, seeing them in other lights, say, as sexual, or funny, or assertive, may seem unfamiliar or indeed, threatening to our understandings of who *we* are. This is very clearly exemplified if we look at instances that work against and challenge those norms. For example, Figure 0.2 accompanied a photographic article in *The Guardian* detailing and illustrating the work of Skateistan, a skating and education project started in Afghanistan in 2007. Seeing images of Afghani women skateboarding disrupts the norms of their traditional media representation in the West and makes those images all the more remarkable.

Another example is the *Persuasion* project by photographers Idris and Tony which presents images of Asian men as unabashedly 'masculine, sexual and desirable', again working against the familiar with regard to their representation within mainstream media – and especially advertising – in the West (Cheney-Rice 2014). Why should it be that such images are so startling and unfamiliar? And whose interests does it serve to replicate the same old images week in and week out?

That raises questions of course about who has the power to control the representations that *become* familiar – and so we see

Figure 0.2 Skateistan volunteer Erika ollies in front of the destroyed Buddhas of Bamiyan, which were built in the 6th century but blown up by the Taliban in 2001. Image courtesy of Skateistan

how all of these things are tied up in that 'circuit of culture'. Media representations are a cultural issue, but they also have huge political, historical and social repercussions. Their study has been seen as important as a way of highlighting and beginning to address imbalances in the cultural and media representations on offer within societies. Much analysis has taken as a start point a void in representation and called for an increase in the visibility and variety of representations. Only once that has been achieved does it seem we can argue for 'better' and more nuanced representation (Branston and Stafford 2010). Real parity of representation or 'representational adequacy' to borrow a term from the museums literature (Bennett 1995), is found when viewers/readers/players/visitors are offered not just positive images as opposed to negative, but 'a range of fuller ways of being imagined, both by others and within the group itself' (Branston and Stafford 2010:121).

Hartley et al. point out that in our shifting and mutating media landscape, 'representative representation' is under increasing attrition 'especially following the rise of interactive, participatory and digital technologies, where direct public *self-representation* can be undertaken by anyone with access to a computer network' (Hartley et al. 2012). YouTube and Facebook are perhaps the most obvious examples (Hunter et al. 2014). They suggest that we may need to shift from a model of seeing representation as 'to' and 'for' people, thinking instead about representation 'with' and 'by' them; this will be explored as a key tension in this book. How might we characterize the representations that are created under the auspices of campaigns such as the Ice Bucket Challenge or #nomakeupselfie (both 2014) that encourage people in front of the camera who might never previously have had the impetus to self-represent? This extension of the discussion into the realm of self-representation gives explanation to the mirror on the front of this book; it is a referent also to representations' power to impact identity and self-image at the level of construction.

Also of interest is exploring what happens after a representation becomes 'public', and in a world of mash-ups and remixes, to some degree out of our control:

> Once a representation becomes public, its career takes it ever further from its maker's intentions. Its symbolism can be *re-presented* (presented again) with completely different meanings.
>
> (Hartley et al. 2012: 153)

An image or text has a life beyond its initial manifestation (see Chapter 6). Hartley et al. use the example of the Statue of Liberty, which was of course produced with a certain set of meanings in mind; optimism, democracy, a heroic vision of freedom. In the film Planet of the Apes its meaning is disrupted, and its direct opposite is true – it becomes a post-apocalyptic vision of despair. In this sense, representation can include elements of copying and parody and is 'promiscuous' across media (2012: 154). It is this that makes it such an interesting site of study.

SOME KEY TERMS

You will read a lot in this book about ideology; that set of ideas that gives us an account of the social world (but normally a partial and select one), a set of ideas that relates to the way power is distributed, and that are often presented as 'natural' and 'obvious'. Ideology connects very deeply with the study of representation. The 'active labour *of making things mean*' (Hall 1982) implies effort, work, action; processes that may all introduce ideological representations. You will also read a lot about identity. Representations, as we have noted, are tangled up with our understandings, and enactment, of identity. Representations serve to disseminate 'nutshell versions of the complex configurations of our identities' (Albertazzi and Cobley 2009: 394). There are many different 'nutshells' that we might conceive of ourselves as belonging to; I am white, middle class, middle aged, mother, wife. The media play out versions of my identity extensively. I am completely unremarkable. But other people may find that the different fragments of their identities on display are far more limited. Or indeed completely absent. Representations circulate and generate identities, teaching us about what other people are like, but also what we should be like, even what is appropriate behaviour for us. They also, simultaneously, are framing how others see us. We assume our identity by adopting sets of codes – gestures, expressions, images, even forms of dress perhaps – that have been 'given' to us. These codes (McQuail 1984) offer fairly unambiguous readings to people from other cultures about who we are and where we come from. They have become established by use and familiarity, and people start to buy into them as shorthand for telling people about who they are. Over time, such representations can become naturalized as common sense understandings, say, of a nation, and of its people, the diversity and nuance of that people lost.

Consider for a moment the range of individuals and characters who are teaching the world about 'Chinese-ness' and what it might mean to be 'a Chinese'. Weibo phenomenon Guo Meimei. Actors Jackie Chan and Zhang Ziyi. Model Liu Wei. Artist and activist Ai Weiwei. Entrepreneur and billionaire Jack Ma. The legendary figure Fa Mulan. Anybody who is Chinese will understand that this is a very limited range of representations. And it might not be too much to imagine that those from other geographical contexts would understand that it is a limited offering also, especially when one takes into account the population of the country stands at nearly 1.4 billion. But over time, and through repetition, representations start to stick.

This might all seem rather innocuous. So what. But representations are of course very closely bound up with issues of power, and thus remain significant. What might it mean to be rendered invisible? Or to see yourself played out in the media in ways that are alien to you? This is why it matters what terms like man, woman, black, white, gay, straight, able-bodied, poor, mother, father, partner and the like *mean* to us. There are issues of power at stake, as will be seen throughout this text.

Representation also demands we acknowledge the audience, latterly seen as a much more active state of *being*. If audiences are equipped with the ability to be considered in their responses to, or even to reject, the meanings of media output, then that gives us pause for thought. Devereux asks 'if audiences are active agents in the construction of meaning why should we bother to analyse content at all?' (Devereux 2007: 188) It's a good question. Hall's encoding/decoding model of audience reception (1973), where media producers construct meanings and encode them into texts, but where audiences can decode them in a range of ways (accepting the preferred reading, negotiating a reading that accepts some but not all of the message, or reading it in a completely oppositional fashion), allows a space for the study of representation. If texts are even in part authored by readers themselves, if they are never finished until they are consumed and have potentially infinite meanings (McQuail 1984), then we are already in the process of thinking about representation.

WHAT QUESTIONS DOES THE STUDY OF REPRESENTATION ENCOURAGE US TO ASK?

Analyses of representations are far-reaching, encouraging the exploration of a number of questions of crucial importance as we consider the role of cultural texts within our diverse and dispersed media ecology. What and/or who is represented in a text? What is absent? Who is silenced? Would it ever be ok to have three men on a radio programme talking about a woman's right to have an abortion? Such a debate at Oxford University was cancelled in 2014 after criticisms from campaign groups that it would feature only male speakers (Mashhour and Murphy 2014). What is the relationship between the different representations on offer in a text? This encourages us to think about power relations – Are they equal? who is seen to hold the authority? Whose viewpoints are privileged? Are all representations the same or do they conflict? If so, is that conflict a productive and useful one? How do texts try and position the viewer, visitor, or reader in relation to meaning? Are you supposed to sympathize with a character or perspective? Fear them/it? Understand them/it? Whose eyes are audiences encouraged to see through? Why is one particular representation chosen over others? What are the alternatives? And are there always alternatives? Are audiences being encouraged to think in a certain way about a topic or people? And to exclude other ways of thinking? For example about sexuality, mental health, crime or age. What languages are being utilized? What discourses are being activated? What do they reveal? And how might we decode them? Also, critically, we need to take a temporal perspective, asking questions about how and why particular forms of media representation change over time. This is very important. The representations on offer might 'improve'. Of course, they also might get worse. Finally, as you read this book, I'd like to propose that you consider the following question: Is it time to worry less about representation?

Might the endless obsession with Disney films and their representations of gender (the very stuff of the tedious 'Media Studies is a Mickey Mouse Degree' critique) be missing the point that the media *can* be quite good at shattering stereotypes as well as re-enforcing them? Is this an argument that has been won? Should we be content with the range of representations that are now on offer to us? Or accept that under the auspices of irony anything goes? What I hope is that this book will give you the tools for articulating how and in what ways the issue of representation remains meaningful in our changing – and challenging – mediascape, and in the face of the increasing number of case studies that force us to re-examine the field.

STRUCTURE OF THE BOOK

This book is written to work in complement with seminal texts on representation. Hall's *Representation* (1997), later re-worked as Hall et al. (2013), gives a comprehensive overview of 'the work of representation' at the level of meaning making; semiotics, discourse and subjectivity. Webb's *Understanding Representation* (2009) traces the uses of the term and in so doing, establishes why and how it has come to be so difficult, yet so pervasive. Prendergast's *The Triangle of Representation* similarly does a fine job of recounting that complex lineage and outlining its theoretical terrain. These are incredibly useful perspectives, and are essential to our understandings of representations and their real world consequences, but in 2016 they only tell us part of the story. None of these texts take as a point of exploration the changes within our media environment at both the level of production and consumption. Here, digital and social media are integral to all of the chapters, being an unavoidable, and intriguing, area of study in the field.[1] The book's approach thus embraces a mixed-media ecology and works across it, whilst acknowledging that reliable and fast internet access is far from a global reality. Where possible the book incorporates a global perspective, using international examples and challenging those studying the media to think outside of their traditional understandings of what constitute 'the media', 'the cultural' or 'the creative' industries (my previous use of the word 'visitor' three times may have done that already).

The opening chapter introduces a variety of theoretical frameworks within which we might begin to study representations and their significance. It uses the works of key thinkers in the field to explore some contemporary cases, setting the tone for the chapters that follow. The chapter looks at representation from five perspectives: representation and reality; representation and myth; representation and visual culture; representation and persuasion; and representation and identity politics. This last section introduces a number of avenues for exploration which will be at the nexus of the book; representations of race, gender, sexuality, class, age and disability. The politics of representation as they relate to such markers of our identities are of course layered and not universal, and are enmeshed with, say, our discussion about self-representation or discourse. You will therefore find them interwoven within each of the chapters in the ways identified below.

Chapter 2 asks questions about how language is implicated in the construction of the discursive formations central to circulating ideology and power in our societies. Using the seminal works of Foucault, the chapter goes on to focus on two underexplored areas within the theory of representation. First, the part that silence plays as an intervention within discourse, and second, the way that discourse is constructed within social networks, specifically the micro-blogging platform Twitter. Issues such as trolling are raised here as particular discursive problematics within such spaces. Within the chapter, the politics of representation are opened up with regard to how transgender people are constructed within mainstream media and discourse.

In Chapter 3 the focus moves to the abundant opportunities for self-representation that are now enjoyed by vast swathes of the world's population online. It begins by defining self-representation then looking at social networking sites as particular frameworks for the construction and presentation of self (referencing Goffman 1956). This chapter more than any other raises questions about the adequacy of traditional theories of representation to account for what is happening within our new media ecology, segueing into questions about self-promotion, and critiques of neoliberalism and the attention economy. The chapter explores these questions looking at the phenomenon of the 'selfie' (and associated campaigns such as #nomakeupselfie or #icebucketchallenge) and the anatomy of a Facebook page. It references the inevitable challenges to privacy, democracy, authenticity and permanence that are now frequent areas of debate in academia, but also media discourses more broadly. The chapter comes with the caveat that there are many who remain disenfranchised from these practices of self-representation by nature of their continued exclusion from such spaces (the digital divide).

Chapter 4 concentrates on another complex site of self-representation in the form of reality television. The representations under discussion in this chapter are intimately intertwined with questions about celebrity, consumer culture and surveillance, and force us very explicitly to tackle the relationship between representations and 'real life'. How might we understand the truth claims that are made within the reality genre? And how might the vast range of sub-genres of reality television complicate that picture? The chapter focuses in part on the new breed of structured reality programmes that now pepper our television schedules and streaming services, and connects those with the discursive online communities that are dedicated to fandom for such output. Representations of class and gender in particular are scrutinized in the case studies presented, but also in the poisonous wider debates that circulate around these 'ordinary celebrities' (Grindstaff and Murray 2015).

This is contrasted in Chapter 5 with a look at the larger representations constructed within society about who we are and where we come from with a look at mediatization of the past. This breaks down in two ways. First, as a study of mainstream textual outputs; television, film, radio, but also newspapers, books and video games. Second, the chapter gives an introduction to the museum as a site of complex representation, implicated in the construction of identities, nations, and Others variously defined. It remains uncommon to think of museums as media, but the chapter is predicated on that idea; museums are communicators, storymakers, constructors of discourse, and of what can be known about a subject or a people. In their practices of collection, classification and (especially perhaps) display, they are implicated in the construction of meaning. It is of critical importance that we challenge the accepted wisdom that museums are neutral, a-political and even 'safe' spaces, that we ask questions about the kinds of knowledge and authority they construct, and about the silences they construct also. In this chapter, the politics of representing race are starkly brought into focus.

In Chapter 6 the discussion moves to an often ignored but incredibly interesting site for the exploration of representation; subversive and alternative media messages. Here various practices of user-creativity and participatory culture are detailed and opened up for scrutiny through the lens of representation. Playfulness, pranking and jamming are at the heart of many of these practices, and the claims that are made on their behalf are many. Are they symptomatic of a move toward wider and more democratic representations? Do they expose the representational practices of big corporations and advertisers as cynical and tired, unfit for our complex new mediascape? Are we empowered to imagine ourselves, our communities, and our politics differently within alternative media discourses? And how does the mainstream respond to – and deal with – resistance? This chapter is a fitting conclusion in a book where the complexity and fragility of our systems of representation is so apparent a theme.

This book cannot claim to give an exhaustive exploration of all aspects of the study of representation. Such study takes many forms and has a temporal dimension; its accounts alter over time. Instead, I hope this book encourages readers to reflect on the ways they are implicated in the circulation of ideas, images and discourses in our culture(s), and that it gives them insights into how those representations – and their implications for society, politics and culture – might be unpacked.

NOTE

1 For a readable and balanced introduction to the wider issues at stake in any consideration of digital media (including social media) I recommend either Naughton (2012) or Taylor (2014).

1

THEORIES OF REPRESENTATION

There are many theoretical debates that circulate around and complicate the concept of representation. This chapter outlines a number of these discussions, introducing a range of high profile thinkers whose works should form the basis of any study of the media and culture, and whose ideas remain seminal to the unpacking of representations in particular. I am not able to comprehensively outline their contributions here – that has been done extensively elsewhere, and the original texts are themselves the appropriate source materials – so instead this chapter offers insight into how those theories might be applied to contemporary cases, and how the associated languages and tools can be combined in the analysis of 'everyday' representations. The chapter is split into five discussions, each building on those preceding it: Representation and reality; representation and myth; representation and visual culture; representation as persuasion; and representation and identity politics. The sum of these parts is not a comprehensive account of the origins of representation studies in philosophy or art history (say) but a set of discourses that will emerge again in the chapters that follow, sometimes problematically so. A number of case study texts are introduced as a way of grounding the discussions and making visible the theory as applied to practice. At the heart of this theoretical engagement with representation is the realization that:

> We live immersed in representation: it is how we understand our environments and each other. It is also how we both *are*, and how we understand ourselves; representation is implicated in the process of *me* becoming *me*.

> (Webb 2009: 3)

Implicit is a recognition that representation is constructive, resilient, and implicated in the forging of identities, cultures, communities and in the articulation of difference. Representation is no straightforward window on the world, as will be demonstrated over the following pages.

REPRESENTATION AND... REALITY

In the introduction it was noted that representation is concerned with the construction of meaning, and a number of examples were explored that demonstrated the complexity of that. The discussion is extended here with a more detailed look at how 'reality' is constructed in media and cultural texts through the use of signs and codes, and so features a brief sojourn into semiology, and an overview of Stuart Hall's 'constructivist' approach to representation (1997).

According to Jonathon Bignell, 'one of the most powerful ways of thinking about media has been the approach known as semiotics (or semiology)' (1997: 1) and Daniel Chandler notes in his *Introduction to Semiotics* (available online) that 'semiotics is often employed in the analysis of texts' (2014). In the media, of course, a text can mean many things – not only written or traditionally 'textual' materials. According to Chandler, a text can be any 'assemblage of signs (such as words, images, sounds and/or gestures) constructed (and interpreted) with reference to the conventions associated with ... a particular medium of communication' (2014). It is the 'assemblage of signs' that is of interest here, and by extension, how audiences or readers (for example) attach meaning to those assemblages.

Semiotics, based on the foundational ideas of Ferdinand de Saussure (1959) and Charles Sanders Peirce (1894), helps us to understand language and its operation. The approach has since been extended to the study of other cultural texts; the media, fashion, theatre, and video games for example. Semiotics rests on an understanding that the words, language and other signs which we use in our everyday and social contexts help to shape our reality. This sounds relatively innocuous, but has been a revolutionary philosophy because it implies that 'signs shape our perceptions, rather than reflecting a reality which was already out there' (Bignell 1997: 6):

> language and the other communication systems which we collectively use, provide the conceptual framework in and through which reality is available to us.
>
> (Bignell 1997: 6)

So, language *creates* our concepts of reality rather than reality existing before language gives words to it. The words we use for things – the linguistic signs (whether spoken or written) are, according to Saussurean semiotics, 'arbitrary' (Saussure 1959). There is no *real* connection between how a word sounds or how it looks on a page and the thing it describes. However, as much as the connection is arbitrary, we tend to use the words we are given through our language and our culture. Thus, there is no deliberate choice available to us about what a sign will stand for, and our decision to use the words given to us is not a conscious one. We learn how to use word-signs at an early age, and we don't question them. Charles Sanders Peirce said 'we think only in signs' (1894: 10) – in words, images, smells, sounds, flavours, objects – but these things have no meaning until we assign such to them.

According to Marcel Danesi, representation can be 'characterised as the process of constructing a form X to call attention to something that exists either materially or conceptually, as Y' (2008: 116). But balancing the equation X=Y is not straightforward. Whoever has constructed text 'X' had or has intent, a historical and social context, an agenda, and so on, which are complex factors which *should* enter the picture when we try to deduce meaning. The purpose of semiotics is to study these factors, and to try systematically to come to an understanding of *how* X=Y (Danesi 2008), and under what circumstances. In Saussurean semiotics, it is the coming together of signifier and signified (the form and the idea) which gives us the sign. There is a difference being marked here between the form and the conceptual level of meaning making, and the connection between them is, as we noted, arbitrary. These connections are instead dependent on context, and on social and cultural cues. In the introduction when we examined the symbolism of the poppy, this is the difference that was being highlighted.

The world is of course full of different signs, and the next stage in our exploration of meaning making requires us to think about the relationship between them. According to Ferdinand de Saussure, every sign acquires its value 'by virtue of its difference' from all of the other signs in that system (1959). The word-sign 'table' only has meaning to us because we can differentiate it from words such as 'chair' or 'lamp'. Without such difference, it could not function as a sign.

So, what does all of that mean to media semioticians? Media students and scholars are interested in establishing what systems are in operation that, in sum, give words, images, news reports, films and memes (for example) particular meaning, and differentiate them from others. It is only through these processes that the differences between man/woman, life/death, black/white can be constructed and understood. As was noted, Saussurean semiotics posits that concepts are defined not positively, in their likeness to one another, but negatively, in contrast (1959). Signs are grouped together into codes which construct meaning, and this is of great interest to those interested in culture; dress codes, genre codes, typologies in music, film or graphic novels for example. So, the pop music code will have familiar ingredients that come together in a recognizable way to create something that differs from rock music (which has its own code). Another example of a code system can be identified in the practice of tattooing. Cultural identity, military experience, gang affiliations, past convictions and even music tastes can all be inscribed on the skin through particular motifs and symbols that can be – that are designed to be – incredibly complicated for 'outsiders' to interpret. Such bodily modification is culturally and socially encoded and practised, and its undoing, through tattoo removal, is a practice of identity re-appraisal and recuperation.

What matters in all of this is the separation of form and content. If the message of a text, its connotations, can be separated from the form, then the choices that are made about the particular images chosen in a newspaper report, the actors in a drama, the props on a set, the words that are used, all of those things become loaded. None are incidental or accidental. They are charged with ideology, invested with power, markers of difference, and carriers of 'value'. The choices we make about the signs we present and the codes we utilize matter.

So, we start to see how signs and codes work to indicate meaning in texts; to construct a version of reality or a narrative, and to present certain things as logical and natural, and by extension other readings as illogical, nonsensical, or invisible. Marcel Danesi argues that we need to ensure future generations are able to understand the historical and signifying forces at work in the operation of the media 'factory' (2002: 216). 'Simply put' he says 'it behoves us to make sure that our children will be able to distinguish a meaningful news documentary from an ad for running shoes' (2002: 216). I would extend this to say that in an era where more and more people make and distribute their own media – where representations and self-representations are ubiquitous – we should *all* be encouraged to think about how our own contexts, ideas, prejudices and inevitably partial world-views filter into and frame the representations we construct, shaping the codes and conventions that we utilize in order to construct meaning therein.

Such a view of meaning making processes fits within what Stuart Hall has called the constructivist approach to representation. This approach recognizes the codes and conventions that have been overviewed here, and 'acknowledges that neither things in themselves nor the individual uses of language can fix meaning in language'. In this view, as we have seen 'Things don't *mean*: we *construct* meaning, using representational systems – concepts and signs' (Hall 1997: 25). According to Stuart Hall, representation is a very different notion to that of reflection because it implies 'the active work of selecting and presenting, of structuring and shaping ... the more active labour of making things mean' (1982: 131) rather than just presenting them, as it were, at face value. This allusion to 'active labour' reminds us that there is nothing natural or inevitable about representations, they are the product of 'work'; they are works of construction. This approach informs and shapes discussions throughout this book, and underpins the extension of semiotic analysis into the realm of myth in the following section.

REPRESENTATION AND ... MYTH

In the 1950s, French semiotician Roland Barthes drew attention to the value of the tools of semiotics for the study of media and popular culture in particular. He was interested in the relationship between what is seen, and what is understood at the level of myth; in the distinction between what he called the *denotations* and the *connotations* in a text (1957). Saussure's theories allowed us a way of thinking about denotation as a process, and Barthes gives us a way of thinking about the connotative functions of representation. One very clear demonstration of the distinction between connotation and denotation comes in the 'active' work of logos; for example, the Apple logo. At the denotative level of the sign it might be said to be solely a representation of an apple, nothing more. But we all bring many more associations with us to our reading of the Apple brand than that. Apple products are often understood to be desirable, with smooth lines and slick design. They are expensive, and for people who are ahead of the curve; early adopters perhaps. These are the associated connotations that make up the brand personality of Apple. Apple is of course a divisive brand however, and the logo might equally connote a set of more negative associations for you. Perhaps you see Apple users as posers, or as unimaginative followers of the latest hardware trends. That is of course not what the company wants you to think when you see the sign, but as we now know, media messages can be rejected, our readings subversive (Hall 1980). Either way, we can conclude that the Apple logo is not just apparent. It cannot be read simply at the denotative level as *an* apple. It means something at the level of connotation; a myth has been created about the brand and its products.

These connotations come from our various social and cultural experiences and knowledges, and are, in part of course, informed by and reflected in the media and advertising. Barthes called this phenomenon, the bringing together of signs and their connotations, the making of 'myth' (1957). To Barthes, a range of implicit narratives are embedded (knowingly or otherwise) in the texts that we consume. Through the making of myth, signs, the X=Y relationship that Marcel Danesi encouraged us to look at, becomes more complicated. In this model, existing signs are made to function as a signifier on another level; at the level of the ideological. These myths are not always easy to spot, and so often go unchallenged, seeming to be intuitive, natural, common-sensical; and therein lies their power. According to Barthes, many of these mythic elements have become so naturalized and widespread in media representations that we hardly see them any longer. Myths such as the struggle for good over evil, the need for heroes and the loss of women's innocence are a case in point – things we encounter all of the time in film, tv and advertising, but don't always 'see' (Barthes 1957). The study of mythology involves trying to locate and identify signs, showing how they are built into codes, and analyzing how these structures work to communicate certain messages over others – other messages which are silently excluded (Bignell 1997). We begin to see how ideology can creep into media texts. How they have layers of signification, and can, unwittingly often, be involved in a process of naturalizing or normalizing certain messages, and neutralizing others.

One lense through which myths have been analyzed and made visible is Edward Said's concept of Orientalism, one of the founding ideas of Post-colonial studies (Bowman 2012). Orientalism is a term coined by Edward Said in 1978 to give name to the processes by which Western media outlets manufacture representations of the Middle East and East Asia. According to Said they present sets of stereotypes again and again in order to produce the Orient in the minds of consumers in particular ways; as simultaneously backward and exotic, most notably in the many harem scenes depicted in art, and, we might note more recently, in filmic treatments such as Disney's *Aladdin* (1992), *Alexander* (2004) and *Black Gold* (2011). Orientalism is, according to Said 'a Western discourse about the orient that is biased, condescending, misrepresentative and interpreted solely through the eyes, words and media of non-native onlookers' (2003). Said understands 'The Orient' as a semi-mythical construct that is intensely problematic in representational terms. The Middle East is understood as little more than an arid landscape, as in Dreamworks' animated biblical film *The Prince of Egypt* (1998, Figure 1.1).

In recent years (especially since 9/11) attention has turned to the representation of Muslim cultures and communities in particular. Muslims are depicted by mainstream Western discourses as a homogenous group, incapable of independent thought and inherently backward in perspective; not least when it comes to embracing democracy and rights for women (Morey and Yaqin 2011).

It has been noted by Chris Weedon in her study of identity and culture that;

> In much Western discourse on Muslim countries and communities, the language used reflects this assumption that only Western values and standards are valid. Such discourse is also marked by a homogenization of the Muslim 'other'.
>
> (Weedon 2004: 139)

So, Muslims are represented through processes and practices of 'Othering', understood as one community, one culture; one

Figure 1.1 The Prince of Egypt, 1998, Dreamworks

riddled with the 'problem' of terrorism. There has been a shift in recent years so that Islam has been allotted the role of 'chief bogeyman' in Western news, a group of 'irrational fanatics' easily led astray by authoritative male leaders (Barker 2012: 267). So, as a result, 'any reference to Muslims is likely to switch on the notion, implanted by numerous other stories, that most Muslims are terrorists and/or fundamentalists in their interpretation and practice of their faith' (Parekh 2000: 169). This is done in news stories in subtle and not so subtle ways. Markers of difference are located in the very language used which associates 'them' with irrationality, fundamentalism, an ancient and overly paternalistic and draconian value system and legal system, derogatory attitudes toward women, and as a people literally 'cloaked' in mystery. 'The Muslim' is marked as a visible, yet simultaneously curiously invisible and inaccessible, threat. We can see here how we move from denotation, to connotation, and to myth, and by extension, to the personal and political ramifications that might be felt by (in this instance Muslim) groups and individuals as a consequence. We are reminded again that representations are constructive; they frame and feed into our understandings of the world and our place within it. This is the case for the language we use which plays into particular discursive frameworks (the subject of Chapter 2) but is also true for the images that are allowed to circulate within the archaeologies of knowledge associated with a particular topic (Foucault 1969).

REPRESENTATION AND ... VISUAL COMMUNICATION

Image analysis is relatively new, especially given more than 30,000 years of visual message production (Lester 2010: 115). This is in part, Paul Lester says, due to the fact that, in the early twentieth century at least, photographers were undermined or considered to be 'reporters with their brains knocked out' (Lester 2010: 116). It was not until the second half of that century that Roland Barthes, amongst others, showed us the importance of visual literacy. Visual communication can be understood as more ambiguous, suggestive, and open to multiple interpretations than other forms of communication, not least because the codes that are utilized remain unspoken, are not pinned down in language, and are non-textual. According to Jostein Gripsrud, 'images are composed of elements that are not as clearly distinguished as the word-signs of verbal language. The meanings of images are therefore often unclear, fleeting or plural' (Gripsrud 2006: 32).

Machin and Mayr make a few suggestions as to how we might think about the connotative functions of images: First, that the more abstract an image is, the more overt and foregrounded its connotative communicative purpose. Second, that whether the communicative purpose of an image is primarily denotative or connotative depends to some extent on the context in which the image is used. Third, that what an image connotes may, in some contexts, be a matter of free association, but that for the most part, where image makers need to get a specific idea across, they will rely on established connotators which they feel confident their target audiences will understand (Machin and Mayr 2012: 50–51). This last point is especially applicable to advertising as we will see in the next section.

First however, we might note that, when it comes to the analysis of any media text at the level of denotation or connotation, and of images in particular, *context is everything*. There are a number of different contexts within which we should understand the use of an image (here I am drawing on Lester 2010). First, in its presentational context; where does an image appear? A portrait, for example, means something very different depending on where it is found or mounted. The portrait of musician Tinie Tempah (by Nadav Kander, 2011) which hangs on the wall at the National Portrait Gallery in London, appears in a very different presentational context to a portrait concealed in a locket worn around someone's neck. An image's potential readings are dictated, in part, by their mode of presentation. Second, we should think about an image with regard to its production context; how is it physically produced and under what circumstances? An image of an individual produced for an advertisement or a magazine may look very different to a picture you take and display on Instagram or that the paparazzi might take outside of a nightclub. Third, we should think about an image's historical context. An image can mean a different thing depending on when we look at it, and how we understand the historical moment within which it was produced. So, for example, when looking at images of Oscar Pistorius, the connotations associated with the multitude of photographic representations of him have changed over time. As a Paralympian he has been admired for his strength and speed, and became a visual icon of the 2012 Olympic Games. But after his trial and subsequent imprisonment his public image is forever altered; our readings of his image are changed. This diachronic view of representations is a particularly revealing one. Fourth, we should think about an image in the context of other images: Is it one amongst many? An image in a photo album or in an exhibition is asked to enter into a relationship with other images. In other contexts, with graffiti on a wall for example, our capacity to limit or control the way our image appears amongst others might be part of the game. In a newspaper, an image on a page will have a relationship with the text around it (captions, the article), but also perhaps the other articles and adverts that surround it. Here we are noting that images are rarely consumed in isolation. Lastly, we should think about the context of reception. Our reading of a text may differ depending on other factors, such as our location (in a library or on a bus perhaps), who we are with, whether our friends, families, or by ourselves. We might also argue that the range of experiences and ideas that we bring with us to our reading of a text will affect what we take away from it. So, for example, our experiences of growing up, family, joy, trauma, plus our sexuality and other identity attachments, are likely to impact on our reading of an image of a man and woman exchanging rings on their wedding day.

Many of the images I've referenced here are photographs, and it is worth thinking for a moment about the photo as a particular kind of media text. Photojournalism is of course not something we tend to teach any longer on journalism and media courses in any traditional sense. We might note the massive proliferation of photo in all aspects of our lives; the photos we take and share, the photos we are sent, that we are tagged in, and the photos we 'consume' in the media. In some respects, there is no longer anything 'special' about a photo, and thus a photographer. A photo perhaps does not have the same aura and authenticity that it might once have had by virtue of its scarcity. Walter Benjamin explored this fully in his essay on visual texts in *The Work of Art in the Age of Mechanical Reproduction* saying 'Even the most perfect reproduction of a work of art is lacking in one element: its presence in time and space, its unique existence at the place where it happens to be' (Benjamin 1955). Digital photography has of course massively amplified the trend toward mass production and the proliferation of images. In that landscape it is easier to consider oneself a photographer, but at the same time, perhaps harder and harder to take a photo that stands out and might be considered 'good' in comparison to others. We might note also that the nature of the photos that we see in the media and journalistic output have changed. There remains of course a role for considered and reflective photos from warzones and the photos in periodicals like *National Geographic* continue to be striking. But this is also, lest we forget, the epoch of the paparazzi; an age where a blurry image of Britney Spears eating lunch, or Kate Moss getting out of the car, often receives more attention. We might also note the increased capacity for 'creativity' in photos' production, post-production, and use. That is, the opportunity to manipulate them. Given all of that, we might say that it is more important than ever that we think about the relationship between a photograph and reality – how far is it fair to say that a photo is a window on the world?

Photography used to be understood as 'a purely physical-chemical cause and effect system, untouched by human hands, and consequently an "objective" representation of whatever was in front of the camera.' But in actual fact:

> the photographer has to make a number of choices, of framing, point of view, lenses, lighting, film, speed, etc. – plus all the choices in the darkroom [not so much now – but post-production certainly]. Put together, all of these choices provide the photographer ... space for her or his subjectivity.
>
> (Gripsrud 2006: 30)

So we are reminded that representational texts, in our case here images, are constructed. They do not just capture reality, but help to shape it within the frame. Images tell multiple stories – some of them perhaps more 'true' or at least more 'authentic' than others. Given that conclusion we might ask why we feel so squeamish about the use of airbrushing in photography, a squeamishness that was demonstrated in the column inches given over to discussion about Kim Kardashian's attempts to #breaktheinternet in 2014. Airbrushing is big business, and computer-mediation of photographs is becoming ubiquitous; just look at the rise of an app like Instagram, or a program like iPhoto. Anyone who has used them will know that it takes little know-how, and no time at all, to alter an image quite considerably, and prepare it for distribution, with potentially global reach. However, for some reason, we seem to view this element of computer-mediation, when used in the mainstream media, as analogous to lying, as if photographs were ever 'true' in the first instance. This is of course problematic, as Jen Webb proposes: 'How can we say something is a misrepresentation if its obverse, perfect representation, does not exist?' (Webb 2009: 36). We might only conclude that 'partial, contingent representations are the best we can achieve' (Webb 2009: 37).

In 2015, there are a number of emergent forms of computational visual representation that we are talking more about in media and (particularly) journalism studies. Data visualizations are now a core staple of news media provision, in papers, periodicals, on television, and especially on the web where they become animated and interactive. Such forms bring together images, symbols, tabular and graphical content and text in order to tell stories that have their origins in data. We have seen a 'broad reaching, and often uncritical fascination with data visualisation and its potential for knowledge generation' (McCosker and Wilken 2014: 155). This quote is revealing; the use of data visualization techniques is not solely about finding more aesthetically pleasing ways into big data analysis ('beautiful data': Segaran and Hamerbacher 2009), but about 'knowledge generation', actually changing something in the world. McCosker and Wilken go on to caution that whilst being aesthetically pleasing, data visualization techniques can be 'experienced at such a scale and speed that comprehension is difficult', which can in turn reinforce the sense of a subject as 'unknowable' and alienating (2014: 159). We have yet to fully understand what the impacts of the computational turn will be in representational

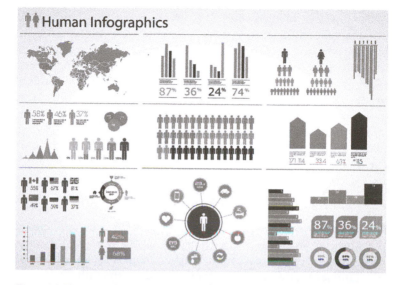

Figure 1.2 Human Infographic © Antun Hirsman/Shutterstock.com

terms, but infographics strike me as particularly interesting for a number of reasons (see Figure 1.2).

Infographics, as Megan Knight (2015) notes, are not new, dating back to the late nineteenth century, but in recent years they have become more visually complex, and more interesting for those studying representation, not least because, necessarily perhaps, they have to revert to very simplistic imaginings for how to present things like people, difference, geography, cause and effect. There are a limited number of elements from which they can be drawn given that their impact needs to be instantaneous. Lev Manovich, in a 2010 piece on data visualization called such graphical elements 'graphical primitives' that are necessarily reductive (Manovich 2010). That use of the word 'primitive' is enlightening; the representational elements are often unsophisticated and old-fashioned even though the technologies employed on the back-end might be considered 'cutting edge'. We need to think more about the implications of what is shown within such graphics, and what remains missing. Can an infographic tell the whole story? Can it be manipulated? How are they interpreted or 'read'? Our understandings of these questions are very limited at this stage, but are of consequence not least because 'the presentation of information in data form can have its own weight, regardless of the actual value of the information or its impact on society' (Knight 2015: 70). Think for example of the infographics utilized in the reporting of election campaigns and results; their very presence can seem to indicate the consequential nature of the story and its legitimacy, when often the data they rely on is speculative or partial at best. Here we begin to see how representation can spill over into persuasion.

REPRESENTATION AS ... PERSUASION

It is a truism to assert that in 2015, advertising is everywhere. In the street, in shops, on public transport, in the post, in our social media spaces, on the web, in the papers, magazines and television programmes that we consume. Yet it is, curiously, rather absent in the detail of peoples' lives; an advert is according to Guy Cook, 'everywhere but nowhere': 'never the programme [people] are watching, never the letter they are waiting for, never the website they are seeking, not the part of the newspaper they are reading' (Cook 2001: 1). As such, ads are a 'peripheral creation' (ibid.). But when you speak to people about their attitudes to advertising, feelings run high. Many people regard them as a genre too closely entangled with the values of capitalist consumerism, globalization, and the market. Perhaps only a few would confess to regarding adverts as high quality artistic output, as clever, funny and entertaining in their own right. Yet whatever our stance, adverts can certainly be memorable, conjuring associations, much in the same way that music can. They also bleed into other aspects of our lives, in material ways (as merchandise such as the Compare the Meerkat toys[1]), in the ways we express ourselves (as catchprases), and the soundtracks of our lives (as in jingles). Guy Cook has said that 'Ads use fictions, word play, compressed story-telling, stylized acting, photography, cartoons, puns and rhythms in ways which are often memorable, enjoyable and amusing' (Cook 2001: 3). They are incredibly – and increasingly – sophisticated, a nod to the personalization of advertising in recent years affirms that.

Adverts do of course have an even more fractured relationship with 'the real' than many of the other texts we work with in media and cultural studies. We might be cynical about the claims they make, knowing all of the time that they serve a very particular purpose, to persuade us to consume: To part with our cash; to be somebody newer, better, healthier; to buy into (literally) lifestyles, ways of viewing the world, and product. As such, we might indeed surmise that adverts 'lie'. But the persuasion at work is often far more ambiguous than that. It is in more subtle ways that advertising seduces us; through associations, often unspoken, just hinted at, and we as consumers fill in the rest.

One example that demonstrates this ambiguity well is Facebook's first ever commercial, released to celebrate reaching the landmark of its billionth user. The central message of the advert is that 'Chairs are like Facebook', a message that was widely ridiculed on its release in 2012. The advert, a very cinematic and (one can assume) expensive piece of media, featured a series of colourful images and short films of chairs, some empty, and some with people sitting in them. The full text of the advert's voiceover is as follows, and do note that I am not naïve to the fact that I am re-producing it here out of context:

> Chairs. Chairs are made so that people can sit down and take a break. Anyone can sit on a chair, and if the chair is large enough they can sit down together, and tell jokes, and make up stories. Or just listen. Chairs are for people. And that is why chairs are like Facebook. Doorbells. Airplanes. Bridges. These are things people use to get together, so they can open up and connect, about ideas and music and other things that people share. Dance floors. Basketball. A great nation. A great nation is something people build so they can have a place where they belong. The universe. It is vast and dark, and makes us wonder if we are alone. So maybe the reason we make all of these things is to remind ourselves that we are not.
>
> (Facebook 2012)

In this advert the ludicrousness of some of the associations and metaphors we buy into through advertising is starkly brought home to us. Here we see it is not a lie that Facebook tells, but instead a set of abstract associations are set up to connote the myth of community online, and of Facebook's centrality to those processes. The talk of nations, which on first viewing seems rather jarring, does of course echo the many proclamations at the time that if Facebook were a country, it would be the third largest in the world by population (Williams 2012). The myth being connoted here is of connection, togetherness and belonging; this is the kind of nation we should aspire to be a part of. The idea that Facebook could be compared to a chair or a doorbell – inanimate objects without any agenda – is of course a spurious one. As critic Antonio Lopez surmised at the time, 'Those are objects that lack a systemic, corporate agenda that tracks its users (sic) interests and then sells them as commodities' (Lopez 2012). He goes on:

> Imagine the chair you sit in monitors all the activities of the room you're in and the conversations your (sic) having with your friends. The chair then compiles that information and sells it to other chairs so that when you enter into other spaces, the chair forces you to sit in a particular position so that you see ads or through a window that you had no intention of looking through. What if the chairs re-arranged themselves to encourage you to sit with particular people that you didn't intend to sit with? I imagine that we wouldn't like these chairs very much.
>
> (Lopez 2012)

Lopez alludes to an uncomfortable extension of Facebook's community ethos and structure with regard to advertising and persuasion; that the various algorithms at play have rendered advertising increasingly personalized in response to the trails of data that we leave in our wake in such spaces. Facebook is of course interested in community because it has monetized it, not for altruistic reasons or an interest in our personal growth or social justice (per se).

So, how might we get to the rub of what an advert is saying to us, and to what it might *mean* to us as potential consumers? In analyzing an advert, we might start by thinking about the textual form it takes. Is it a paper ad, a billboard or on the tube? Is it a television advert or a film trailer? Here we foreground the medium and not the message, indeed, as Marshall McLuhan famously noted, the medium *is* the message (1964). This is important to note as it tells us much about the context for reception – will it be seen at a passing glance or by a captive audience? What you do to catch somebody's eye will of course vary in different formats. We might list the signs that are present. Are they iconic? Are they symbolic? We should think about their juxtaposition; how they have been positioned in relation to one another. What is the story being told here? We might ask what cultural codes and assumptions are being drawn on? How familiar will they be to people? Or are just certain people (for example sports fans, or gardeners, or women) being targeted? Whose realities are being presented here? Whose are absent? What are the implications of that? It's also worth spending time considering the technical effects that have been used. Why this angle and not others? What is being foregrounded? Does an advert use close-ups? Who of? What music is used? Are there special effects and editing tricks? We might also identify other relevant historical and cultural contextual information (there's that word again – context). Advertising, although a relatively young medium, has changed dramatically in the last 50 years or so.

Following Barthes' analysis of myth we should also seek to unearth the narratives being created and the myths constructed. Is this a story about sex? About self-improvement? About being a man or a woman? A mother? An employee? A patient? Is this a story about fitting in? About being a family? About being well? Is it supposed to be funny? How is it supposed to make you 'feel' (think for example of adverts asking you to pledge donations)? Does it use testimonials? Is there a 'science bit'? That might bring us to thinking about what the preferred reading of this text is and to ask what other readings of the text might be possible? Is it open to interpretation?

All of these questions can help us begin to expose how an advert works as a specific representational text with intent. But any study of advertising, and indeed other media, soon brings us to the issue of identity politics; questions about the ways in which particular social groups have been made visible (or indeed rendered invisible) within the mainstream.

REPRESENTATION AND ... IDENTITY POLITICS

This chapter has demonstrated that in all sorts of ways, representation has a frustrated relationship with reality. That ambiguity renders representations intensely political and searingly troublesome. The use of one image over another in a newspaper article for example, or one word-sign in place of an alternative, is to align with a world-view that is never neutral, and to naturalize a particular ideological stance, often working to further entrench it. As Nick Couldry identifies:

> Social order is not a given or natural state; it is constructed practically and represented symbolically, and media representations of the 'order' of social life help enact and perform that order.
>
> (Couldry 2012: x)

To say that something is political is to note that it can never be neutral or a-historical, even when it might appear to be ambivalent. A case in point is the umbrella. It might seem difficult to imagine an umbrella as being political, as *meaning* beyond the core value that is found in its functionality as shelter. Yet in 2014 we saw the umbrella become politicised within the context of the Hong Kong 'Umbrella Revolution'; the yellow umbrella in particular became the internationally recognized symbol of the protests. Something that looks innocuous to you might be understood as suggestive and troubling to somebody else.

Representations as they relate to race, class, gender, age, disability and sexuality are notoriously and historically problematic. It is not controversial to assert that in Western contexts at least there has been a privileging of white, middle-class, hetero-normative, and often male, perspectives within the media and broader cultural output. I will overview briefly some of the problems of representation and some examples in the closing pages of this chapter, but bear in mind that these themes will be revisited variously throughout the book.

For representations of class, it has been argued that images of working-class identity in particular have been broadly negative and derogatory (Skeggs 2004, Wood and Skeggs 2011). As David

Weltman notes, to be a worker and a thinker is very rare in media representations (2008). We have seen hateful representation in the press of an 'underclass' of welfare cheats, dole bludgers and those unwilling to work. In the US, the stigmatization of 'Trailer Trash' in programmes like *The Jerry Springer Show* has been comprehensive, and in the UK at least, we have seen the demonization of 'chavs' and their distasteful habits of consumption (Hayward and Yar 2006, Jones 2011, Devereux 2014).

Representations of gender remain some of the most problematic (Gill 2007). Strong, interesting, female characters in series like *Sex and the City* sparked debate about how far we thought we had come when it first aired in 1998, only it emerged in time that all the characters really wanted to do was get married and to shop. In the late 1990s the pneumatic Lara Croft (1999–) had everybody talking about what would be at stake as gender representation went virtual. There is the long-standing issue of pornography and the recent extensive trolling of feminists of both sexes online. Associations continue to be made: women, girls even, as beauty queens, objects to be consumed; men as strong and rational, aligned with technologies, business and finance.

Representations of race and ethnicity have been of interest to cultural theorists and commentators for many years (see for example multiple chapters in Philo 1999). In some realms, representations of race and ethnicity were abundant – in museums and galleries for example – where whole communities were depicted as Other, exotic, and manifestly different in great big exhibitions. In other arenas, there seemed to be a complete *lack* of representation (on TV or in advertising for example), apart from perhaps in the news where black and minority ethnic groups were over-represented in stories about crime (Gomes and Williams 1990, Stabile 2006, Cushion et al. 2011), or as dependent on aid. In 2014 in the UK, there were discussions about the latest offering from Bob Geldolf's Band Aid collective in aid of the Ebola crisis (Band Aid 30's *Do They Know It's Christmas?*) which was widely considered this time around to be both patronizing in its efforts, and offensive in its lyrics (versions were also produced in France and Germany). This gives us insight into how and in what ways a diachronic study of representations might be helpful; looking at how they change over time demonstrates that what is acceptable in one time-frame might cease to be acceptable in another. Representations are unstable, moving and open to re-negotiation, as this example demonstrates.

Again, with respect to homosexuality, we have gone from a complete absence of representation to an abundance; not least because capitalist entertainment industries cottoned on to the idea that the 'pink pound' was worth courting. But we might again ask whether *any* representation will do? Campness is still an indicator of gayness in much media representation. Very often gayness is still represented as a 'problem' of sorts, not least in the way it is reported in stories about sport. Bisexuals remain largely invisible from the mainstream media.

Representations of disability similarly have been problematic. In 2012 we saw more media focus on people with disabilities than we ever have. The 'super-humans' we met during the Paralympics continue to fight for a lasting legacy on how we view disability (Hodges et al. 2014, Jackson et al. 2014). Since then we have had the extraordinary trial of Oscar Pistorius which of course pivoted around his disability and is discussed in Chapter 4.

Age is an interesting site of study also. Younger people in news reports tend to be associated with particular types of crime – mugging and stabbing for example – and we are disturbed by how far young people have become defined through technologies, and other acts of consumption. Simultaneously there is always a worry that society – and the media – are robbing people of their youth. Forcing them to grow up too quickly. Yet if old age is anything like it looks in the media, why would you want to? Older people are often seen as bad tempered, senile, and dependent, although, now we have an aging population, internet-savvy, with money in their pockets, there is suddenly a race to court them into the cinemas.

There has been some talk of a 'metanarrative of progress' over the years (Harris 2006) noting that, broadly, we might have seen some improvement in representations in line with an increased awareness of identity politics. Geraldine Harris is suspicious of any such claims:

This metanarrative often embraces a sense of having gone 'beyond' identity politics, even as events in the world of the social have continued, repeatedly and violently, to put them back on the agenda.

(Harris 2006: 2)

To take for a moment representations of lesbians and gay men, we might conclude that increased visibility has not necessarily equated to vast progress in representational terms, refracting the real-world problematics of queer politics. There were a number of media reports in 2014–15 which attested to the continued power of representations of the gay kiss in particular to destabilize media organizations and their audiences; in the US (Huffington Post 2014), Austria (BBC News 2015c) and Angola (BBC News 2015d). Such representations matter to people (who respond positively or negatively) because they are tied up with the ways that we see and understand ourselves and our own identities. As Paul Bowman asserts: 'mediation and media representation arguably has profound effects on all levels of culture, right down to the production and reproduction of the most intimately felt senses of identity' (Bowman 2012: 66). The consequences and power of representations then are profound, and we will see throughout this book how they become battlegrounds for struggles over meaning within society, over what is deemed acceptable, what is unsayable, what is punishable. Another recurrent theme will be the ways in which identity politics plays out through the body, for as Jen Webb notes, 'the body is not just an organism; it is a cultural performer' (Webb 2009: 80). The politics of identity are a sub-thematic of every chapter that follows, starting in Chapter 2 with a study of discourse, and a detailed look at the troubled representation of trans people.

NOTE

1 Merchandise associated with the comparethemarket.com campaign 'Compare the Meerkat'.

2

LANGUAGE AS POWER

This chapter explores a number of questions related to language and the various discursive formations that circulate within society. How do our linguistic interactions link into larger discourses, and in turn, to ideology? What do they tell us about the balance and circulation of power? And how might we begin to unpack all of that through discourse analysis? The chapter's initial focus is on pinpointing what we mean when we talk about discourse, and working through its potentials as related to issues of power using the works of Michel Foucault in particular. The latter part of the chapter focuses on silences as interventions within discourse, and on the circulation of discourse within the Twittersphere, a vibrant – yet incredibly complex and conflicted – discursive community.

WHAT WORK DOES DISCOURSE DO?

Marianne Jorgensen and Louise Phillips say that 'underlying the word "discourse" is the general idea that language is structured according to different patterns that people's utterances follow when they take part in different domains of social life' (2002: 1). So, in different realms of our social lives, we will interact with people according to a range of linguistic codes and utterances that are known to operate within that framework. For example, in the Houses of Parliament in London, in the European Parliament in Brussels, or the White House in Washington, we expect people to use a 'political discourse'; in an SMS or Facebook update, we expect people to use rather informal discourse and even 'text speak'. Discourses are 'like "social scripts" we perform' (Storey 2012: 131). In this chapter we will see that there are complex and ideologically charged factors at play in the ways such discourses are constructed, used and interpreted within different contexts.

There is in fact no common sense or accepted definition of what discourse is and of how it might be studied. John Richardson asserts that 'Discourse is a very trendy word referring to a very trendy concept. It is one of the most well-used (some would say *over-* or *mis*used) words in academia today' (Richardson 2007: 21). With that in mind, we should be wary about how we use this term, and recognize that just as some choose to take a very narrow understanding of what it means, others might take a much broader approach. Richardson chooses to locate it in instances where at least two sentences are in dialogue with one another, each anchoring the meaning of the other, and suggesting common sense interpretations of the text. Following our discussion in the previous chapter, we might note that such interpretations are not neutral; they are based on the particular forms of social and cultural knowledge that we have at our disposal. It is we, ultimately, who make any two sentences or ideas work in discourse (Richardson 2007).

To broaden our discussion from the particular to the general, we might also understand discourse as being active in constructing whole topics, giving us a language for talking about, say, immigration, which works within ideological frameworks and contexts (as in 'political discourse'), In this sense, discourse is, according to Stuart Hall, 'a group of statements which provide a language for talking about – a way of representing knowledge about – a particular topic at a particular historical moment' (Hall 1997). Note how Hall says 'a way' not 'the way', 'a language' not 'the language'; one language amongst other possibilities which are generally side-lined. Jorgensen and Phillips define discourse as 'a particular way of talking about and understanding the world (or an aspect of the world)' (Jorgensen and Phillips 2002: 1). Such a definition allows for the macro-level study of discourse, in the wider sense of the word, and the micro-level analysis. It also implicates the processes of production (talking) and reception (understanding) in the flows of discourse. Taking a constructionist approach to language means, according to Richardson, recognizing that it is: social in that it exists in a dialogue with society – being produced by it, and helping to re-create it; context specific in that how we use it is contingent upon our social contexts and locations, in a bar, a university seminar, or an interview for example; linked to identity, allowing us to present a version of self that we feel is aspirational; full of assumptions (whether consciously or not); active, always and inevitably seeking to *do* something in the world whether arguing, persuading, informing, explaining, exposing, supporting, detracting or attacking; infused with power, recognizing that certain ways of speaking – and voices – have more power than others, both power *in* discourse and power *over* discourse; and intensely political, its use has an agenda (Richardson 2007).

One demonstration of the potential of discourse to 'act' and to 'do' is the speech act as particular discursive intervention; a form of performative communication (Austin 1962). Here the direct consequential nature of discourse is best exemplified. In speech acts, the utterance of particular words changes something in the world. So, on one's wedding day, saying 'I do' is not just an utterance, it actually enters you into a legal partnership with somebody. Arriving in a country and saying the words 'I claim asylum' indicates the pursuance of the status of refugee and enters an individual into the asylum system; a particular set of procedures and protracted conversations (Jeffers 2011: 31). Speech acts in themselves function. In these examples they do something very profound. We might conclude then that discourse can be incredibly powerful. But let us not forget, discourse is also contingent, contextual and can change over time. It is for this reason that witness statements can never be taken at face value, and might differ dramatically from person to person. This is a reminder that we always should look to determine the context within which a discourse originated and operates, and to review it in light of our findings.

Let's take an example, looking at a number of utterances from UK Politician Nick Clegg. To provide some context, Nick Clegg is a Member of Parliament in England, and is ex-leader of the social-liberal Liberal Democrats party, who, between 2010 and 2015 were in a coalition government with the centre-right Conservative Party in Westminster. One of Nick Clegg's enduring legacies will no doubt be his now infamous policy U-turn on university tuition fees in England, which, under the Lib-Cons coalition, rose from £3,000 per annum to £9,000.

In April 2010, just before the general election Nick Clegg signed the Vote For Students pledge to 'vote against any increase in fees in the next parliament and to pressure the government to introduce a fairer alternative' (NUS 2010). This pledge (popular of course with those of university age who voted in unprecedented numbers for Clegg's party) was clearly undermined by the policy interventions that followed. Nick Clegg, who subsequently became the Deputy Prime Minister in the Coalition Government, later voted in favour of a rise in tuition fees and said in November 2010 that:

> In politics just as in life, you sometimes discover there are things that you wanted to do that you are not able to do... I hope that when people look at the details of what we are doing, they will see ... it lowers the burden on the vast majority of students.
>
> (in *Telegraph* 2010)

The change was met with protests on the streets, a series of petitions, and an uncomfortable time for Nick Clegg in front of the cameras. By 2012, Clegg had the following to say: 'We made a pledge, we did not stick to it, and for that I am sorry... It was a pledge made with the best of intentions – but we should not have made a promise we were not absolutely sure we could deliver' (in Wintour 2012).[1]

We might surmise then, that somebody saying something on one occasion cannot be taken to represent their opinions in any consistent manner. In beginning to analyze this example, we do well to ask under what conditions the initial pledge was made, and how those conditions had changed by the time of the second utterance, and third. What functions and purposes did they achieve, or aim to achieve, in their particular contexts? In the first instance, we might speculate that the intention was to get people to vote for the party. As an aside, we might like to think about a pledge as a speech act: What kind of commitment is being made, and just how binding is it?

Another example is the case of English author Hilary Mantel's comments about the Duchess of Cambridge (formerly known as Kate Middleton). On 18th February 2013 historical fiction writer Mantel gave a lecture at the British Museum for the *London Review of Books* on 'The Royal Body'. The Press picked up on a few of her comments, stirring up a debate that became nothing short of vitriolic. The *Telegraph* online led that evening with the headline 'Hilary Mantel portrays Duchess of Cambridge as a "shop window mannequin"' (Furness 2013), and the following day the *Daily Mail* led with 'A Plastic Princess designed to Breed' saying:

> A best-selling author who has based her literary career on writing about the Royal family has launched a bitter attack on the Duchess of Cambridge.
>
> Hilary Mantel used her position among the novel-writing elite to make an astonishing and venomous critique of Kate.
>
> (Infante 2013)

Later that day UK Prime Minister David Cameron even became drawn into the debate commenting in Parliament that Mantel had been 'completely misguided' in her comments (BBC News 2013).[2] Mantel's response, via a spokesperson, was to urge people to read or listen to the speech itself 'because it puts everything in its full context' (in Brown 2013). To look at the actual text of the lecture – all 5,000 words of it – begs a different interpretation of the text. Actually, Mantel was very sympathetic toward the Duchess, seeking to comment on the very fact that royal bodies are so open to scrutiny by the media and the public. She concludes:

> We don't cut off the heads of royal ladies these days, but we do sacrifice them, and we did memorably drive one to destruction a scant generation ago. History makes fools of us, makes puppets of

us, often enough. But it doesn't have to repeat itself. In the current case, much lies within our control. I'm not asking for censorship. I'm not asking for pious humbug and smarmy reverence. I'm asking us to back off and not be brutes... The pen is in our hands. A happy ending is ours to write.

(Mantel 2013)

A rather different message once one looks at the context. Of course I am not naive to the irony here; readers might wish to reflect on the particular extract I have re-produced here and ask questions about how it has been abstracted from its originating context in this representation also. What does my selection tell you? What do you know about my agenda?

As demonstrated here, in media, journalism and cultural studies we use discourse as a concept with which to explore the 'struggle for meaning' at the level, for example, of the words chosen for news reports, the phrasing of interview questions on political panel shows, the wording of policy documents and press releases. It is discourse analysis that many media scholars turn to in order to study such phenomena. Discourse as framed within the news media has been a particular focus of research giving valuable insight into such things as the representation of black and minority ethnic groups in the media, or the framing of gender and disability. Such analyses start from the point that 'the "content" of newspapers is not facts about the world, but in a very general sense "ideas"... language is not neutral, but a highly constructive mediator' (Fowler 1991: 1). As such, as Fowler notes, 'The world of the Press is not the real world, but a world skewed and judged' (Fowler 1991: 11). Through the analysis of discourse, we can get to grips with meaning making, communication and language, social interaction, and knowledge construction. It is a broader approach than traditional textual analysis, seeking not simply to quantify the uses of terminology or other textual features, but to locate them within their context. It is possible to look at the detail in the language used, and analyze how it points to the kinds of persuasion being done and to the broader ideas being promoted.

More recently, there has been talk of the Critical Discourse Analysis approach, one that is specifically interested in the political implications of language choices (Wodak and Meyer 2009, Fairclough 2010, Machin and Mayr 2012). Here, the analysis is carried out with specific reference to the societies that produced the discourse, and to position it in relation to the societies that are constructed as a result. It is this link to social and political elements that renders it *critical* discourse analysis. For the most part, this is the kind of analysis that we are looking to achieve, asking questions about how discourse is used (consciously or otherwise) to create, re-create or obscure inequalities and/or domination. Sociopolitical context is key.

DISCOURSE AND POWER

We have noted that representation is ensnared in the broader circulation of knowledge and power. In Michel Foucault's work on the subject, this was seen as critically and politically important:

> What I mean is this: in a society such as ours, but basically in any society, there are manifold relations of power which permeate, characterise and constitute the social body, and these relations of power cannot themselves be established, consolidated nor implemented without the production, accumulation, circulation and functioning of a discourse.
>
> (Foucault 1980: 93)

For Foucault, discourse was about more than mere language. It was a way of framing a set of knowledges and statements about a particular topic, in a particular moment, which became the dominant frames within which that topic was then understood. Discourse was thus infused with power, as Storey neatly summarizes: 'Discourses produce knowledge and knowledge is always a weapon of power' (Storey 2012: 132).

Discursive formations that Foucault unpacked in his analyses relate to subjects like madness, sexuality and punishment (1979, 1981), which he felt only existed 'meaningfully *within* the discourses about them' (Hall 1997: 45). The discourse constructs the ways in which a topic will be understood, and its repetition across multiple representational texts and within varied institutional contexts consolidates our understanding; partial and perspectival though it might be. As such, discourses are indelibly entwined with our readings of power, and senses of our own agency and autonomy. To Foucault, the relationship between discourse, knowledge and power (via 'truth') is clear, and gives the study of representation renewed real world application:

> In the end, we are judged, condemned, classified, determined in our undertakings, destined to a certain mode of living or dying, as a function of the true discourses which are the bearers of the specific effects of power.
>
> (Foucault 1980: 94)

Discourse produces certain conceptions of, say, sexuality, that have real effects for individuals and the ways they operate within different realms of experience, and are given permission to operate. Even if not true, a discursive formation can sustain a 'regime of truth'; 'the types of discourse which it accepts and makes function as true' (Foucault 1980: 131).

Power, according to Foucault, functions not in a one-way hier-archical system but circulates within society, not necessarily residing in the state, the ruling class or monopolies, but something we are all implicit in making function – we are all caught up in systems that enable it to circulate. To Foucault, power circulates in the private as well as public spheres, in the family as much as in the state; a micro-physics of power can be found at the level of the everyday and the localized. At this localized level, power is rooted in our beha-viours, bodies and relationships in ways that are not merely straightforward projections of the dominant classes (Foucault 1980).

For Foucault, it was in the body ultimately that we find this micro-physics of power made manifest; the body being produced according to different discursive formations – for example about sexuality, gender and violence, or our understandings of what is appropriate behaviour. The body itself becomes a site upon which different regimes of power and knowledge write their meanings and effects (see Hall 1997 for more on this). So Foucault encourages us to think about representations within the wider discursive formations within which they belong – a variety of contexts; institutional, historical, social and political – and to think about how power circulates around and through us even at the level of our own bodies.

To explore this further, I want to look at the politics of representation as they relate to trans people and communities. In a society where gender is seen as bipolar (male/female) and identifiable in our very bodies, it is common to view transgender individuals as deviating from norms that have become naturalized. Representations are often seen to indicate that to be transgender is a 'disorder' that must be 'treated'. This is no better demonstrated than in the treatment of Caitlyn Jenner, the American reality TV star and former athlete, who transitioned in 2015. The story is understandably perhaps very enticing with its link to the Kardashian family, but the reporting was often ill-informed and insensitive, not least as it was often accompanied by pictures of Jenner's pre-transition self (for example in Dodge 2015). At a Comedy Central Special attended by two of Jenner's daughters (taped on 14th March 2015) there were three separate instances of comedians making jokes at her expense although two of those were edited out of the programme that aired (Yandoli 2015). On 30th March at a different ceremony, actor Jamie Foxx made another joke about Jenner's transition (Vanmetre 2015), and news reporting following the 'Call me Caitlyn' *Vanity Fair* front cover came in for heavy criticism (Nelson 2015). So why is it that the level of public discourse around gender dysmorphia is so parlous? Some recent articles can help to demonstrate the 'regimes of truth' that are put in place around gender, and to highlight the problematic nature of discourses about what it means to be transgender in particular.

In February 2013, in the UK's *Daily Mail*, there appeared an article by Richard Littlejohn headlined 'To boldly go where no man's gone before...'. It responded to a move from trans groups in the UK to argue for gender-neutral toilet facilities. Here is a section from the opening of the article:

> You can't say you weren't warned. I told you the 'diversity' brigade wouldn't rest at gay weddings... the trannies have regrouped... The number of gender-specific categories is mind-boggling... why should

the rest of us have to put up with toilet arrangements designed to cater for such a tiny minority?

(Littlejohn 2013)

Let's have a look at some of the discourse in play here. The article makes reference to what it calls an 'equality industry' of lobbyists who are launching something of an assault on the values and sensibilities of 'the majority'. The 'trans crowd', are presented as 'mind-boggling' in their complexity, and unreasonable in their demands. They are asking for 'special treatment', and seeking to undo a 'historic' distinction between 'Gentlemen and Ladies' loos'. The tone is flippant, and the language is loose. To 'prefer not to say' what one's gender is is nonsense. According to Littlejohn to be transgender is to be different from the 99.99 per cent of the population; from 'the rest of us' (a very clear 'us' and 'them' distinction is evident throughout). 'They' are a tiny, but very noisy, minority; nothing more than a nuisance but with the most 'militant, vociferous campaigning group in the country'. So, we begin to see how the discourse of 'gender', blurred here unhelpfully with discourses about 'sexuality', is framed with particular reference to transgender people and communities. Another more disturbing example from earlier in 2013 can demonstrate this further. On 13th January, again in the UK, Julie Burchill wrote an article for *The Observer* in defence of her friend Suzanne Moore who, having made a remark about Brazilian transsexuals, had been attacked on the microblogging site Twitter. In that article, Burchill said the following:

a gaggle of transsexuals... the trannies... a bunch of bed-wetters in bad wigs...

To have your cock cut off and then plead special privileges as women – above natural-born women, who don't *know* the meaning of suffering, apparently – is a bit like the old definition of chutzpah.

(Burchill 2013)

Burchill's piece unashamedly uses the available and incredibly limited repertoire of language choices such as 'Chicks with dicks' and 'shemales' in order to refer to trans people; referents that are no doubt familiar to readers and signify a set of assumed shared discourses. She does so in an attempt to recontextualize a set of events. Instead of a community rightly concerned about their (limited) representation, trans people become a 'gaggle'; disorganized, noisy, cackling, and impotent. The rhetorical devices being used serve to dehumanize the trans community. Again, the piece appeals to a 'majority' which is seen to unite in a weariness at the boldness, brashness, visibility and voice of those who fight for the rights of transgender individuals. Soon after, the article was removed from the website, as were the thousands of reader comments that it had amassed. Of course, it is virtually impossible to unpublish something on the web.

It is clear that the language used in these texts could be seen as anti-trans and bigoted; representing identification as transgender as 'other', abnormal, absurd yet threatening, a performance that goes against the hetero-normative gendering of the body. If we think about those whose research explores gender dysphoria, and who seek funding in order to investigate new – and sometimes controversial – treatments for transgender people, including children, it is difficult to imagine that their job is made any easier when the state of public discourse on the subject is framed within the media in such derogatory terms. In 2011 Trans Media Watch made a submission to the Leveson Inquiry into press ethics and practices in the UK which looked at the relationship between the British press and the transgender community and surmised that it demonstrated 'unethical and often horrific and humiliating treatment of transgender and intersex people by the British press', treatment that seeks to 'mock', 'intrude', 'scare', and 'monster' with 'disastrous' results (TMW 2011). A damning appraisal indeed. According to the report, trans people continue to find it difficult to find and sustain jobs, often suffer physical and verbal abuse, endure family breakdowns, and suffer health risks in trying to conform to societal expectations. A 2015 BBC report claimed that 41 per cent of transgender people in the US have attempted suicide compared to 1.5 per cent for the general population (Morris 2015). Some of the burden of responsibility for this parlous situation, according to Trans Media Watch, must fall to the press: 'The media – and the tabloid press in particular – has played a powerful role in creating and sustaining a climate of prejudice against transgender people' (TMW 2011). The *Guardian* reported in March 2015 that many trans women were living in fear and hiding their true identity by reverting to presenting as male: 'If transwomen have to hide to be safe' Zach Stafford asked, 'what does progress look like?' (Stafford 2015). By looking at the actual word choices in the two examples detailed above we can relate that evidence to wider sociopolitical issues, elucidating our understandings of where power resides and how and in what ways people are *dis*empowered also. The treatment of trans people within our health systems, our penal systems and our education systems (discursive domains Foucault paid special attention to in his analyses) continues to be problematic, and discourse is not innocent in the maintenance of that scenario.

On screen, we might note that there have been a number of much more positive and rounded portrayals of transgender people in recent years. Louis Theroux's 2015 BBC documentary *Transgender Kids* is a sympathetic treatment of the subject,[3] and Laverne Cox's recurring character Sophia in Netflix's *Orange Is the New Black* might be considered another case in point.

Episode 3, dedicated in part to Sophia's backstory (directed by Jodie Foster), gives us insight into Sophia's transition from being

Figure 2.1 Laverne Cox as Sophia in Series 1, Episode 3 of *Orange Is the New Black*, Netflix, 2013

Marcus, a married firefighter with a son, Michael, and what she has given up in order to facilitate it. Transitioning has been a long and costly road for Sophia, in financial terms, but also with regard to her freedom; she was imprisoned when her theft of credit cards was uncovered and her son reported her to the authorities. We see just how stark the consequences of disempowerment can be for those who have transitioned when Sophia's medications are withdrawn in a display of power by the authorities. It's worth noting that when it came to filming her pre-transition scenes, Cox, as a woman who has herself transitioned, was ruled too feminine for the role and consequently her twin brother agreed to step in and play the part.

Laverne Cox has noted how limited the range of trans characters has been in the past, often, typically, consisting of characters who work in street economies such as sex work. So,

> When [OITNB] came along, I thought, what a wonderful opportunity to talk about and highlight issues of trans women in prison. Certainly, Sophia has been one of the most complicated characters I've gotten to play as an actress, and I'm really grateful she's come into my life.
>
> (Cox in NPR 2013)

The following year, in 2014, Amazon launched its own comedy-drama series *Transparent* which tells the story of a transitioning 70-year-old and received much critical acclaim (including being the first online TV show to win a Golden Globe Award – in fact winning two), and in 2015 Oscar winner Eddie Redmayne played the role of Lili Elbe, the first recorded trans woman to have sex reassignment surgery in the 1930s, in an adaptation of David Ebershoff's novel *The Danish Girl*.

Professor of gender studies Jack Halberstam says of this development that it is 'unprecedented in the sense that until 10 years ago if there was a trans character in a film or on TV they were either a problem or a criminal…This humanisation of transgender people is clearly new' (Halberstam in Morris 2015). And so we are reminded of the relationship between discourse and power, and of the dynamism of media representations which change over time, but often achingly slowly.

SILENCE AND POWER

It is easy to equate silence, in representational terms, with invisibility and lack of voice. Yet silence is unpredictable and not easily understood. Consequently, it has been fairly absent from studies of representation, and even of language:

> Within linguistics, silence has traditionally been ignored except for its boundary-marking function, delimiting the beginning and ending of utterances. The tradition has been to define it negatively – as merely the absence of speech.
>
> (Saville-Troike 1985: 3)

There are of course differences between being silent and being silenced within media and cultural discourses, the latter having far more negative connotations than the former (Fivusch 2010). Hesitation, pausing, and listening are all very active non-verbal communications. Silence might also be a consequence of forgetting of course; and our fear of cultural amnesia in relation to such events as the Holocaust makes silence all the more political.

To take a historical approach to, say, the representation of transgender people might be to note that they have had a very limited voice within public discourses, let alone *voices:* the trans community is of course constituted of diverse individuals with varied ambitions and world views. The experiences portrayed on screen and in the press have had very little to do with reflecting the life experiences of trans people, and more to do with Othering and belittling those experiences. Those experiences and voices have been marginalized and effectively silenced which of course has real world political and social ramifications. Other groups we might consider to have been silenced include rape and sexual abuse survivors, and feminist voices also which in recent years, especially in the noisy communications spaces of the Internet, have been not so much silenced as drowned out in a deluge of hate-speak.

In thinking about representation we should be live to such silences, seeking to investigate who is doing the silencing, and to what end. Silence can be a sign of disempowerment and

Figure 2.2 Protester Logan Browning wears tape over her mouth reading 'I can't breath' [sic], Hollywood, California, 6th December 2014. copyright: Patrick T. Fallon/Reuters/Corbis

suppression. But it can also, lest we forget, be a powerful marker in and of itself (see Figure 2.2). In moments of remembrance silences are often employed as a mark of respect, and/or a space for thought and reflection. In such moments, on Armistice Day, or in a sports stadium filled with 70,000 other people, such silences can be immensely powerful statements symbolizing solidarity and unity. Such silences are not safe spaces; they 'speak' and can be the antithesis of neutrality.

One such silence which speaks can be found in the example of avant-garde Composer John Cage's 1952 work 4'33". This composition, at 4 minutes and 33 seconds long, is performed in the absence of musical sound. Performers of the piece essentially do nothing for the entirety of the piece, but it is not 4 minutes and 33 seconds of silence. The audience are encouraged in the act of listening to focus on the sounds of their environment, whatever those might be: the uncomfortable shuffling of other audience members, the sounds of our own and others' bodies, the creaking of our concert halls. We very rarely find ourselves in complete silence, as the piece ably demonstrates. As Jen Webb notes: 'Pure silence, or pure unmediated experience, is not a function of living human beings' (Webb 2009: 11).

Here again we see that silence is not neutral, it can act in the same way that discourse can. In a somewhat ludicrous twist to this particular tale, a story circulated in 2015 claiming that versions of the work on YouTube had had the audiotrack disabled because its use had not been authorized by the copyright owners Warner Music Group. This meme (as it turned out) cleverly drew attention to the political nature of silence; that it can even be owned.

DISCOURSE IN THE TWITTERSPHERE

Social mediascapes offer new opportunities for us to play out – and play with – our identities in ways that are unprecedented (as will be seen in Chapter 3). Much of what happens in these spaces is interesting at the level of discourse, but there are many unexplored questions related to the discursive communities they foster (if such a term is applicable in those contexts). Analyses of discourse within such contexts have begun to emerge (boyd et al. 2010, Zappavigna 2011, 2012, Kelsey and Bennett 2014) but the norms operationalized within such territories are not static over time.

Questions about identity and agendas are abundant, and well-rehearsed within the literature around online communities and 'cybercultures' from the late 1990s and early 2000s. But these spaces have become infinitely more dynamic and as a consequence increasingly complex since that time, not least because of the range of voices that we now find co-located within the same platforms; voices marked by diversity rather than gathered around issues of shared interest and concern as with Internet forums in the past. These are also far more commercialized spaces, and users themselves are commodities whose information has economic value; social media are now awash with marketing material and public relations, for example there is much ambiguity around the voices of celebrities and the extent to which they can be deemed authentic. Questions about what discourse is being asked to *do* within such spaces are of critical importance. With Twitter in particular, a unique discursive community characterized by what Zappavigna calls 'searchable talk', we might also ask how discourse is expected to work across time and space, with individual utterances brought into discourse via hashtags which are used by tweeters in order to anchor meaning and connect with other users (Zappavigna 2011). Other questions arise around the limitations on discourse imposed by the 140 character limit; does such a limit hinder the circulation of discourse, blunt ideas and nullify nuance, or rather simplify our language, clarify debates and sharpen our discourse? Does the hashtag, search capability and associated metadata introduce us to new discourses that we might scarcely have come across before, and thus new ideas and opinions? Does it broaden our discursive horizons? Does the anonymity on offer within such spaces encourage different modes of discourse than might be acceptable in face to face communications? This last question is proving to be one of the more pertinent and troublesome within the Twittersphere, especially with regard to what have been termed 'trolling' and 'flaming' activities; just how powerful is the word of a troll and what are the ramifications of their actions?

High profile instances of flaming and its consequences for individual trolls and their targets have become common news stories. One group that consistently finds itself on the receiving end of such activity is feminist campaigners; best illustrated perhaps by the case of Caroline Criado-Perez in the UK in 2013. Criado-Perez had successfully fought to reinstate a woman on the back of a Bank of England banknote. On the announcement that Jane Austen had been chosen for the back of the £10 note to be released before 2017, Criado-Perez was deluged with rape and death threats, an experience she detailed in a *Guardian* interview:

> 'I'd do a lot worse than rape you. I've just got out of prison and would happily do more time to see you berried... #10feetunder'... 'I will find you, and you don't want to know what I will do when I do. You're pathetic. Kill yourself. Before I do. #Godie'
>
> (Hattenstone 2013)

At one point, according to the Wikipedia summary of events, Criado-Perez was receiving 50 threats an hour. The episode led to the arrest of a number of individuals, but more crucially perhaps, to a Twitter review of its complaints procedure, and the installation of a one-click option for reporting abuse. The incident led many to speculate about the state of attitudes toward women who are visible within the public domain, and who *dare* to intervene in public discourses. This theme has since resurfaced in many guises (including more latterly #gamergate) and led to a DEMOS study on misogyny in Twitter. The study found that between 26th December 2013 and 9th February 2014 (a study period of a matter of weeks) there were more than 2.7m instances of the word 'rape' used in English on the site. Of the UK based study sample of 108,044 instances, the researchers coded a sample and estimated that approximately 12 per cent of these were threatening, so, nigh on 13,000 rape threats in that period. They also found that women were almost as likely as men to use terms such as 'slut' and 'whore' on Twitter, and that 'casual' misogyny (including threats of rape) constituted a high percentage of all misogyny in Twitter (Bartlett et al. 2014). There has been much debate about whether the 'uncivil discourse' of Twitter might in fact be having the effect of 'making us meaner' (Zara 2012).

In Ecuador in January 2015 we got a rare insight into trolling and the power of words from the perspective of a country's President when Rafael Correa used a public address to name and shame users who had authored abusive comments about him on Twitter (and Facebook also). In a three hour address he gave the full names, ages and addresses of three individuals and read out their messages which included a death threat; 'a bullet on your head wouldn't suit you too bad'. He appealed to his supporters to deluge the accounts with tweets. Yet in actual fact, although it is against the law to threaten a politician, the President was also working against the law in his response to the threats. The BBC quoted a legal expert as saying that his address itself raised 'issues of privacy and incitement to violence' (BBC News 2015a). Correa's entry into the discourse was in itself intensely problematic.

Given such examples we might conclude that the discursive community produced within the Twittersphere is one characterized by disempowerment and the closing down of spaces for enlightened debate. But we have noted that power circulates, and has to be fought for and won, and there are plenty of attempts at this within the Twittersphere also; campaigns that start within the searchable talk of Twitter, yet whose influence extends much further when we consider the broader sociopolitical contexts with which they seek to connect. Two examples that we might consider are the hashtags #ICantBreath (2014) and #JeSuisCharlie (2015).[4]

#ICantBreathe was used by hundreds of thousands of people to express their dismay and outrage at the decision of a grand jury in New York not to take a police officer to trial over the death of Eric Garner (see Figure 2.2). Garner was a black American whose arrest following a confrontation with police had been filmed, showing him very clearly saying 'I can't breathe' 11 times before he died, enough to lead to accusations of police brutality. Protesters gathered on the streets of New York and throughout the US to draw attention to injustices being meted out by the legal system (this was not an isolated case at that time, see also #Ferguson in 2014 and the #BlackLivesMatter campaign which originated in 2012). The global use of the hashtag put those in other world locations and timezones in direct commune with those on the streets and enabled them to show solidarity, increasing the profile of the protests, if not their impact. The use of the phrase showed an attempt to empathize with Garner and others who might find themselves the victims of racist injustice, but also connected very vividly with how stifling and suffocating societies and their institutions can be to those from minority groups that remain disenfranchised and oppressed.

A matter of months later #JeSuisCharlie quickly became one of the most used hashtags in the history of Twitter after the terrorist attack on the Charlie Hebdo offices in Paris. The hashtag, which was used more than five million times, was again a way of showing solidarity with those who had died in the attack, connecting with those across time and space who were gathering in diverse locations to show unity in the face of terrorist atrocity. But it also became a way of connecting with a broader resultant discussion about freedom of speech and creative expression; 'I am Charlie'. As an extension of our discussion about discourse within such spaces, we might note how, over time, the hashtag has to some extent been co-opted by those who wish either to vilify Islam, or indeed, to criticize and condemn the ongoing work of Charlie

Hebdo in presenting images of the Prophet Mohammed in satirical cartoons. We might note this as an example of how discourse can alter over time; it is dynamic, spirited and forceful.

It has yet to be established what the worth of Twitter activism might be with regards to real world intervention, change, or awareness raising over time (although see Tannen and Trester 2013 for an introduction to what is at stake). Is it enough simply to show allegiance via a hashtag? Or does this act absolve individuals of being compelled to do *more?* What changes as a result? Discourse might have the power to alter real world perceptions and behaviours over time (for good or ill), but such change is never inevitable. In 2014 there was a very high profile celebrity endorsed campaign to bring home 276 young Nigerian schoolgirls who had been kidnapped by terrorist organization Boko Haram (#bringbackourgirls). *Telegraph* columnist Bryony Gordon said of it in retrospect: 'Nobody really talks about that hashtag any more. It no longer trends on Twitter. It had its moment in the social media sun, didn't work, next' (Gordon 2015). She calls the girls 'the victims Twitter forgot', and notes that such activism has 'the potential … to turn the most solemn of issues into slogans' (Gordon 2015). Within this landscape the power of words is always and inevitably rubbing up against the futility of words. We must be live to the fact that access to these particular discursive communities is not universal – these are conversations that not everybody can play a part in; only 37.9 per cent of the global population use the Internet (internet.org 2014). Nevertheless, these fragile and ephemeral discursive communities are a live site for the study of cultures and how they are produced in and through discourse. This discussion will be revisited in the following chapter which takes as its focus the diversity of opportunities that are being carved out online for self-representation.

NOTES

1 A parody of Nick Clegg's final statement soon appeared online and went viral, the sense among these voters (as portrayed in comments below videos for example) was that they had been either duped or double-crossed, and that Clegg's words were not to be trusted. See 'The Nick Clegg Apology Song: I'm

Sorry (The Autotune Remix)' from The Poke which has been viewed by nearly 3 million people at https://www.youtube.com/watch?v=KUDjRZ30SNo, accessed 8th April 2015.

2   A writer in the *Spectator* said later that day: 'How stupid of David Cameron to join this absurd row over Hilary Mantel's-speech-turned-LRB-essay on monarchy. I strongly suspect that the Prime Minister was told to do so by aides, who for their part had been reading various journalists on the subject, who for their part hadn't actually read the essay at all' (Gray 2013).

3   Although much of the resulting media analysis was startling in its level of misinformation. See for example Carole Malone's *Mirror* article 'Why is NHS money wasted on treating transgender kids who are too young to understand?' 'I'm no expert,' Malone admits, 'But I refuse to believe that any three-year-old is tormented by their sexuality.' http://www.mirror.co.uk/news/uk-news/nhs-money-wasted-treating-transgender-5478956, accessed 8th April 2015.

4   We might also note the #transdayofvisibility in a nod to the previous discussion about the representation of trans people.

3

SELF-REPRESENTATION ONLINE

This chapter focuses on the many noisy, playful – yet still political – sites of self-representation that now pepper our media horizons. Here, the focus is primarily on online forms of self-representation, forms which are often seen as altering the ground upon which media/journalism and culture are being made and consumed, as well as dissolving the distinction between production and consumption. The chapter asks what is at stake when people can create their own representations and distribute them widely, freely and instantly, to a potentially global audience, yet problematizes the celebratory tone of much of the discourse associated with that practice. It begins with definitions before looking at social media sites, and the selfie as a particular kind of self-presentational text. It then goes on to explore the anatomy of a Facebook profile. The chapter questions whether traditional theories of representation are adequate for describing and analyzing what happens within such complex and evolving environments.

Readers are encouraged to reflect on their own uses of online media from the outset here; have they ever posted a video of themselves or a selfie online, have they tweeted, used Tumblr or some other blogging platform? How regularly do they post 'status updates', use the Facebook 'like' or sharing functions? In contrast to other chapters in this volume, it is likely that readers are implicated in the creation and circulation of representational texts within such contexts, not only in their reception and negotiation. This realization will lead us inevitably into a discussion about whether that activity constitutes agency, and if it does, what the ramifications of that might be.

The questions that we might ask about such practices are complex and multiple, ranging from the general to the very particular; focusing on individual sites and the specific frameworks and calls to action that they put in place. Questions emerge such as how do developments in our new media ecology offer *new* models for self-representation? Is representation democratized online? Just because people *can* self-represent online it does not of course follow that they will. What are the consequences of self-representations becoming ubiquitous? Are we in control of our self-representations online, or is any sense of agency in this regard mere illusion? In what ways do commercial interests complicate

Figure 3.1 Diverse Avatars © Janos Levente/Shutterstock.com

self-representation on the Web? And crucially, with regard to the wider topics explored in this book, does the proliferation of self-representations online in turn change representation in the mainstream media? For example, in what ways do our comments or tweets inform the ways that news events are covered, if at all? Are mainstream media genuinely interested in what we have to say about our lives, communities, politicians and interests? And in what ways are our self-representations being utilized, institutionalized and exploited?

Jill Walker Retberg contends that there are three forms of self-representation in the online environment: written, visual and quantitative (2014: 1). This is a proposition that differentiates this context quite considerably from others that are the focus of the chapters in this book. Written and visual forms of self-communication refer to activities such as (respectively) blogs and selfies. Quantitative self-representations reference the multitude of traces of self we leave via activity tracking and surveillance technologies online. Some of that has value to us, such as the value I might find in using a sleep monitoring application, or a fitness monitor such as a Fitbit (and now the Apple Watch). But of course some of that data also has value to others, such as advertisers or governments, and often assumes an economic value for the companies that own it (Retberg 2014; see also Trottier 2012). The latter form of quantitative self-representation is mostly invisible to us, yet an incredible valuable commodity. Written and visual forms of self-representation are the principal foci of this chapter, but I will touch on the quantitive with reference to the business models that sustain and frame the former as activities that have 'use-value' beyond the individual. This means considering the wider consumerist and capitalist ideologies that sustain, say, social networking sites.

FROM SELF-REPRESENTATION TO SELF-PRESENTATION

According to Nancy Thumim, the 'genre' of self-representation tends to involve one, some, or all of the following within the digital mediascape; ordinary people using their own stories and experiences as source materials, and in so doing providing individual perspectives and expressions of their interior worlds. Self-representations are often filmed pieces to camera (often close-ups), photos and voiceovers, and very often have a home-made or DIY aesthetic, although we might note that the softwares we use to create and share these representations become increasingly sophisticated all of the time (see Instagram for example). Importantly though, to Thumim:

> Making a self-representation no longer requires intermediaries to call, invite, edit or prescribe in any way what the text produced will turn out to be. In the online setting people do not need broadcasters to provide a platform, to invite or to edit their self-representations.
>
> (Thumim 2012: 136)

This has become especially true in the online environment where excited talk about democracy and participation has accompanied the rise in opportunities to self-represent to the point where, as Natalie Fenton notes 'the act of digital self-communication has become part of many people's everyday rituals' (Fenton 2012: 125–6). Note that Fenton implicates 'many' people and not 'everybody' here. As we have noted elsewhere, the percentage of people around the globe who are still offline vastly outstrips those that might be considered online, and that is without taking account of access to the reasonably speedy broadband or wifi connectivity necessary to upload and disseminate such content (UNESCO 2013).

We should note however, that there is a long pedigree of creating representations of self that predates our digital environment, and even the proliferation of the mass media as we know it; one only has to think about the many portraits that have been produced over time, and within very differing contexts. Thinking analytically about the presentation of self also has a pedigree. Erving Goffman, writing in the 1950s, articulated a way of thinking about how we present ourselves in social interactions. He saw identity as expressly performative; a performance that differed depending on the context, constituting a process of ongoing impressions management (Goffman 1956). So, to Goffman, it is natural that we behave differently at work to the ways we do with our families or our friends. He proposed that we all navigate both a 'front region' and a 'back region' during such performances. There are things we do, say and make public and there are things we prefer to keep back, to reserve for only a select few, if anyone at all. These things we keep backstage.

> when one's activity occurs in the presence of other persons, some aspects of the activity are expressively accentuated and other aspects, which might discredit the fostered impression, are suppressed.
>
> (Goffman 1956: 69)

Those facets of our character we keep in the back region might directly contradict those that are being presented up front, as in the backstage of a theatre production where the illusions and impressions being crafted on stage might be undone: 'here the performer can relax; he [sic] can drop his front, forgo speaking his lines, and step out of character' (Goffman 1956: 70). Differentiating between necessary or desired performances is something we often do consciously – so, when going on a date, we might decide to foreground certain aspects of our characters and to put others to the background. The same in a job interview. At other times we do it less consciously. Any audience impacts greatly on how we present ourselves, and we read their responses and adjust our representations accordingly in an iterative process of self-construction and presentation.

We can imagine that, in the online environment, these processes have been amplified and given a renewed vigour and complexity (see Trottier 2014). Multiple sites of identity construction have become very much the norm online; sometimes we might foreground certain aspects of our identity (say, on LinkedIn) and at other times, we might highlight different ones (say, on Facebook). Nick Couldry refers to our cumulative endeavours in these contexts as 'presencing';

> a whole set of media-enhanced ways in which individuals, groups and institutions put into circulation information about, and representations of, themselves for the wider purpose of *sustaining a public presence*.
>
> (Couldry 2012: 50)

Such presencing, whether entirely new, or judged as an extension of existing representational media, finds its most high profile expression in the form of the many social networks we now navigate. Social network sites have been made possible by the more dynamic iteration of the web that has been termed web 2.0, a web that enables and encourages community, storytelling, sharing, collaboration and participation, but that emerges from a 'marketing ideology' (Scholz 2008). Within such contexts, our contributions can be understood not only as self-expression but as self-exploitation; we are being put to work, our connective value is being harnessed.[1] The buzzwords often found utilized with reference to social media include dialogue, participation, interactivity, co-production, collaboration, openness, user-generated content, folksonomies and remix. In the sites enabled by web 2.0 functionality and the dynamic code which underpins it, self-representation becomes synonymous with socializing (Thumim 2012) as we operate in 'networked publics' (boyd 2014). To Zizi Papacharissi, this element of social connection not only enables *display* of self but the *promotion* of self as well:

> social network sites enable individuals to construct a member profile, connect to known and potential friends, and view other members' connections. Their appeal derives from providing a stage for self-presentation and social connection. SNS provide props that facilitate self-presentation, including text, photographs, and other multimedia capabilities, but the performance is centred around public displays of social connections or friends, which are used to authenticate identity and introduce the self... individual and collective identities are simultaneously presented and promoted.
>
> (Papacharissi 2011: 303–304)

The link to self-promotion provides a more vivid sense of how social networks and the activity encouraged therein might be linked to a neoliberalist agenda which understands all such sites as potential markets, not least for labour or for attention, ones which internalize the values of the tech scene whose products and services we become increasingly dependent on. This connection is ably articulated by Alice Marwick in *Status Update,* a book grounded in her ongoing research into the high-tech excess of Silicon Valley (Marwick 2014):

Social media applications encourage people to compete for social benefits by gaining visibility and attention. To boost social status, young professionals adopt self-consciously constructed personas and market themselves, like brands or celebrities, to an audience or fan base. These personas are highly edited, controlled, and monitored, conforming to commercial ideals that dictate 'safe-for-work' self-presentation. The technical mechanisms of social media reflect the values of where they were produced: a culture dominated by commercial interest... These changes are deeply rooted in contemporary consumer capitalism, specifically the philosophy of deregulation and privatization known as 'neoliberalism'.

(Marwick 2014: kindle)

Schau and Gilly noted in 2003 the extent to which our practices of consumption feed into our identity construction at every level and this is also demonstrated within our social networking profiles (see Facebook) and practices of self-curation online (see also Pinterest). In such locations most people choose multiple brands and products to associate themselves with as building blocks in the consolidation of a self that they wish to communicate.

The increased interest in what Marshall terms 'presentational media' (2006, 2013) is a fascinating subset of new media studies which, fittingly perhaps, has its origins in celebrity studies. According to Marshall, there has been a shift from a representational media and cultural regime to a presentational one (Marshall 2006), wherein media that is 'performed, produced and exhibited' by individuals can be distinguished from the outputs of the (mostly) large public and private media corporations we have grown accustomed to. Such 'representational texts' as magazines, film, radio, newspaper and TV are seen by Marshall as having a diminished influence within our new mediascape, becoming blended with the 'panoply of other kinds of content' which utilize a 'presentational form of address' (2013). To Marshall 'presentational media' not only characterize our encounters within social media but re-position the self in relation to traditional representational media structures through a process of 'intercommunication' (2006). Marshall has gone as far as to argue for a new discipline of Persona Studies which provides a framework for the study of self-publicization as the 'public self is expanding and proliferating as an increasingly normal activity for a larger and larger percentage of the population' (Marshall 2013: 2). He argues that traditional theories of representation might be fitting for the study of social constructs such as gender and how they impact on identity formation, but that they do not adequately account for the 'agency' of individuals which is so ably demonstrated in the micropublics forged in social media (Marshall 2013: 13). John Hartley echoes this, asserting that we are seeing a shift 'from representation to productivity' not least within the digital environment (2012: 3). We must be careful however not to overextend or overclaim for that agency at a time when the majority of social network users seem content not to push at the bounds of the very limited choices they are afforded within the spaces of the social media gatekeepers. In the new media ecology, as has been noted, traditional imbalances and hierarchies have emerged even in the face of claims to their undoing. The promise of a web 3.0 – a semantic web or Internet of Things – is unlikely to offer redress. A web of data is one where our self-representations will not only butt up against the self-representations of others, but be read, interpreted and given use-value by machines. Within such a landscape individual capacity to act and represent freely will potentially be in conflict with the primacy of a structure of meta-data, and so those interested in genuine agency will need to be able to game such environments, or indeed create their own if they wish to freely 'present'. Such capacity is of course only available to a limited number of individuals, not even all of those who can be categorized as digitally native. Given our current iteration of the Internet, what we know about its direction of travel, and given how (almost) completely commercial interests have shaped the current look and feel of the web, it seems social media are unlikely to take us *beyond* mediation any time soon, regardless of how much we might like to claim them as agents of empowerment and diversity.

FORMS OF SELF-REPRESENTATION ONLINE

This section briefly overviews a (not exhaustive) range of formats our self-representations can take online, from personal websites and blogs, to video creation and sharing activities, dating sites, social networks and the now ubiquitous selfie.

Personal websites, very much in vogue around the turn of the twenty-first century, were most people's first avenue for multimedia online identity presentation. According to Schau and Gilly, they are 'digital collages using symbols and signs to represent and express [consumers'] self-concepts' (Schau and Gilly 2003). Note that the use of the term 'consumers' comes from the original. According to Marwick and boyd, personal websites remain 'highly managed and limited in collaborative scope; people tend to present themselves in fixed, singular, and self-conscious ways' (Marwick and boyd 2010). In 2002, Zizi Papacharissi described the personal homepage as 'a carefully controlled performance through which self presentation is achieved under optimal conditions' (2002: 644). Given that, in the first instance at least (before the rise of in-browser website production platforms like Wordpress), these required a certain amount of technical competency to produce, the commitment needed to self-represent excluded most from the process at that time. Creating a personalized online presence is now more common, and blogs, which presume a more rolling and ongoing communication with the audience, are very much mainstream in 2015. In January 2015 it was reported that there were 220 million Tumblr accounts (Tumblr 2015), and in March 2015 Wordpress were reporting 61.6 million new posts a month (Wordpress 2015). Many such blogs act as personal portfolios and attempts at self-branding (Hearn 2008) – of varying quality (as at www.jennykidd.org). Indeed, with reference to the previous discussion about neoliberalism, we might ask what *is* the difference between self-representation and self-promotion? How did you respond to seeing my own url within these pages? According to Alison Hearn 'Work on the production of a branded "self" involves creating a detachable, saleable image or narrative' (2008: 198). That it is saleable is significant, the self becomes 'a form of property subject to market exchange' (2008: 199). Hosting a blog on a site such as Wordpress does still require above average digital media literacy; it is simply not as intuitive as creating a profile on a site like Facebook or Instagram. Micro-blogging sites such as Tumblr or Twitter are of course easier to use, and provide a more straightforward (in usability terms) and continuous form of self-representation.

Video creation and sharing via sites like YouTube (since 2005, now a Google company) have undoubtedly been one of the most incredible recent phenomena in the realm of self-representation (Wesch 2009). It is easy to forget that the capacity to 'broadcast yourself' (YouTube's enduring tagline) was the preserve of a very narrow minority of mainstream content publishers before that time. Opportunities to make interventions within the media landscape were infrequent and so exceptional as to be the object of significant public interest and academic scrutiny (as with the BBC's *Video Nation* shorts 1993–2001). As of March 2015, YouTube has more than a billion users, and sees 300 hours of video uploaded every minute (YouTube 2015). YouTube is a good example of a company that started very small, but has since become one of the most significant mediators within the global media market to the extent that it has actually spawned a plethora of creative artists who have been mainstreamed, and become one of the most significant players in the advertising arena also. It has a number of revenue sharing agreements with very large media producers and rights organizations, and so has become a space occupied by amateur user-creators and corporate players including advertisers (Burgess and Green 2009). The YouTube channel of fashion and beauty vlogger Zoella is a prime example of how authenticity, self-representation, consumerism and corporate interests are juxtaposed in the social mediascape. Haul videos and unboxing clips are fast becoming some of the most viewed and lucrative on the site, a fact that should be of great curiosity to the media scholar.

To set such activity against, for example, creating a profile on a dating site, demonstrates very vividly how divergent our *goals* can be with regard to our self-representations online, but also gives an indication of how far perceptions about audience shape the representations of self we produce. On a dating site it is an easy assumption that one's every utterance, emoticon (Figure 3.1), image and 'like' will be comprehensively scrutinized with a view to assessing suitability as a mate, and as such, that a profile will be very carefully considered in the making (Fiore 2008, Baym 2010). But given that Zoella's online presentation of self has become her livelihood, it seems a reasonable assumption that she will be equally as shrewd a navigator in the pursuance of an (authentic) 'ideal self' (Ellison et al. 2006).

In 2015, the most pervasive forms of online self-presentation and self-creation are the many social media sites which we inhabit, and which have been referenced elsewhere in this book. These are crucial sites of self-representation and of identity construction and negotiation (Mandiberg 2012). In these locations people choose markers of cool that they wish to adopt and display for an imagined audience of friends and peers (Marwick and boyd 2010). Zizi Papacharissi gives a useful summation:

> social network sites enable individuals to construct a member profile, connect to known and potential friends, and view other members' connections. Their appeal derives from providing a stage for self-presentation and social connection. SNS provide props that facilitate self-presentation, including text, photographs, and other multimedia capabilities, but the performance is centred around public displays of social connections or *friends*, which are used to authenticate identity and introduce the self … individual and collective identities are simultaneously presented and promoted.
>
> (Papacharissi 2011: 303–304)

But they also seek to work across different social spheres, not least the public and private, meaning it can become difficult to compartmentalize seemingly distinct aspects of one's identity within different sites; such as the difficulty I have in keeping my Facebook updates and my Twitter feed distinct. It is not uncommon to draw personal boundaries around the kind of self that one presents within one social network as opposed to the version of self presented in another; here we see the applicability of Goffman's theory within this particular realm of social experience and discourse. Of course, the logic of sites like Facebook is built around forms of 'social convergence' so those distinct selves often become difficult to sustain (Trottier 2012: 2).

It is worth taking a moment to think about why our self-representations are being encouraged in social networking sites. Whose interests does it serve for us to be able to present and network so prolifically within this range of sites (beyond our own interests that is)? Social networking sites are of course mostly run by commercial entities so here we need to think about the political economies of the platforms; how they make their money, who owns them, what or who is being bought and sold? It is no secret that within such sites, it is connectivity itself that has been monetized; the data traffic between people. According to Fuchs, users are an 'Internet prosumer/produser commodity' (2014: 33). Such is the reason that social networking sites ask us to provide personal details in standard templates. This data, rendered as meta-data, has immense exchange value for those corporations to give to advertisers.

> We have an extensive degree of control over the ways we assemble ourselves online and yet the contemporary experience is one of constant negotiation with forces that seeks to disavow their responsibilities to us, and maximise the limitations under which we can act.
>
> (Barbour et al. 2014)

Connective value sells, which is of course why corporations want to sponsor celebrities' tweets or secure their recommendations within such spaces. However, we might note the limited range of options for self-identification that are open to us (with regard to gender, relationship status or educational background for example) to be intensely problematic. Such categorizations might not be compatible with the version of self we are constructing within that space (as 'married', 'single', 'in a relationship' or 'on the lookout' for example), but that is of no consequence to the corporations. There are no doubt competing interests at work; 'the interest of owners may run counter to users' need to differentiate between their various online personas' (Van Dijck, 2013: 200).

No other form of self-representation can have received as much celebration and derision in this landscape as 'selfies' have since they entered the public lexicon in 2012; photos that could be characterized as self-portraits taken with digital cameras or smartphones (see Figure 3.2). The often informal nature of such photos renders them the object of curiosity especially when taken by elites: political, as in the selfie taken by Barack Obama, David Cameron and Helle Thorning Schmidt at Nelson Mandela's

Figure 3.2 Selfie © Yulia Mayorova/Shutterstock.com

funeral (2013); religious, the pope's appearance in a selfie with young people at the Vatican (2013); or celebrities, most famously Ellen DeGeneres' selfie at the Oscars which became the most retweeted photo ever (in March 2014). Academic analyses of the selfie, now starting to emerge, are being carried out along a number of lines familiar to us in our study of representation; what are the socio-cultural ramifications of this rampant form? What does this phenomenon tell us about gender, beauty, fame, youth, power and how it circulates, sex and how it sells, images and how they are constructed (with the use of selfie-sticks now of course)? This might all beg the question: are we becoming obsessed with our online self-ness? If so, does that leave room for anything else? Charges of narcissism and faddishness are frequent in discourse about the selfie, with universally negative connotations with regard to behaviour, and particularly the behaviours of 'the young'. Kim Kardashian's book *Selfish* (released 2015) is a brilliant provocation on this theme, and apps such as 'Everyday' which facilitates users taking a selfie every day in order to 'make a movie of your life', speak to this concern quite explicitly. In February 2015 international media attention fell on Snapchat (an app that automatically deletes posts after a few seconds) after a 16-year-old from Pittsburgh, USA, posted a selfie featuring his murder victim in the background. The story, which was widely circulated on social media, played into discourses about young people, crime and technology, even though, as Psychologist Pamela Rutledge noted in the *Washington Post*, it was really a story 'about criminal pathology rather than technology' (Rutledge in Holley 2015).

Selfies make us uneasy because of the intense centrality of self, that self's hypervisibility offending many people. This is no more true than with the recent trend for after-sex selfies. Taking and circulating such images is seen as a gratuitous form of over-sharing, and looking at them is understood as voyeurism. The circulation of such images on Snapchat, Facebook or Instagram (for example) does raise questions about digital media literacy; are people aware of the longer term ramifications of posting such images? Do they know that many employers now search for job applicants on social media? Do they appreciate that it is virtually impossible to unpublish something online? Or perhaps such a line of questioning overplays the negatives. Maybe the activity should be celebrated for normalizing everyday sex in sites where pornographic representations circulate so prolifically, or for celebrating the consensual in a landscape where the threat of sexual violence is so frequent, or for creating a space for discussion of what happens outside the heteronormative sexual relationship (not least in the many quirky parodic representations that are now being circulated in response).

Cultural critic Trudy (@trudz) holds that charges of narcissism and a lack of respect for the selfie are particularly problematic, but not surprising, with reference to wider identity politics. She notes:

> That women controlling our own images – especially Black women, women of colour, queer women, trans women, disabled women, fat women, poor women (and women whose identities involve multiple intersections) etc. – is met with disdain, claims of narcissism, or even abuse, is not a coincidence.
>
> (Hamilton 2015)

Such accusations might then be seen as a way of responding to the powerful potentials of the form for self-definition and self-representation and seeking to neutralize them. To self-identify as beautiful and interesting in a way that is as hypervisble as the selfie is, according to Trudy, counter to mainstream commercial norms which rely on the self interpreted as incomplete and not quite good enough; self-definition threatens because it 'hurts bottom lines' (Hamilton 2015).

An associated charge relates to the perceived mundanity and insignificance of the representations of self that circulate within the digital landscape; that sense that the activity on 'display' is gratuitous at best, and timewasting at worst. Empty voyeurism. To look at an activity such as the South Korean trend for Mukbang (or food porn) through that lens would be to understand it solely as watching people eat in front of their webcams. Yet the fact that tens of thousands tune in to watch such activity should make us re-evaluate that charge, especially given that South Korea is the most digitally connected country in the world. Might such activity, and the very fact of its prominence in such a context, be a bid for 'remote companionship', or a reflection on a culture that is increasingly image-conscious? As Mukbang star Lee Chang-hyun puts it in a BBC interview 'I eat so you don't have to' (Evans 2015). Dismissing such activity out of hand is not conducive to an understanding of these phenomena.

Tracing the trajectory of self-representations online also brings us to a number of high profile social media campaigns such as #nomakeupselfie for Cancer Research UK (2014), or the ALS #icebucketchallenge (2014) campaign which ultimately went global. In responses to both campaigns – forms of 'selfie citizenship'[2] – there was an uneasiness about the centrality of self, with accusations of competitiveness, narcissism and triviality as inappropriate responses to charity. There have been claims that many who spent time and effort producing the self-representations associated with the campaigns never actually went as far as fulfilling the pledge to donate to the causes. Here we might ask, why self-representations? Are self-representations still synonymous with the authentic (if they ever were)? What makes the selfie so irresistibly sharable? Why are many of us happy to self-represent for charity when we would never dream of doing so at another time? There is much we don't yet know about the value of the selfie, and the many (happy and unhappy) consequences of its appropriation.

This leads us on to noting a number of challenges that are presented by such platforms with regard to self-representation. First, the decision about which 'me' to be within such contexts can be baffling in the extreme, and managing our range of self-productions in different sites can be labour intensive. Second, they raise questions about the extent to which our privacy remains important to us and should be preserved. Is being public not private the new social norm as Mark Zuckerberg would like us to think? In 2014, a number of celebrities found their intimate self-portraits going viral following instances of hacking and exchange (termed #TheFappening, not unproblematically). Jennifer Lawrence, the most vocal of the victims, asserted that the leak itself was a 'sex crime'. It would appear that we want to have the circulation of our self-images only on our own terms, but the default of the Internet as open, and the ability of able hackers to work around our privacy settings means that self-representations are rarely our own exclusively. In 2011, LinkedIn was in trouble for allowing images of users who 'liked' a company to be used in advertisements for that company without the subject's knowledge. As a response, LinkedIn anonymized the people, but their images remained. Allied to this is the issue of whether we can delete our self-representations, and under what circumstances. It is not always as simple as we might think it should be. Or is that just what companies like Facebook want us to think so we don't pursue them to remove content? On Facebook, it's virtually impossible to terminate an account without first manually deleting every bit of content. You can deactivate the account but not remove the account from its servers.

An associated challenge concerns the extent to which we understand the permanence of the self-representations we produce within such landscapes, and their accessibility by others. A 2011 survey revealed that 91 per cent of employers now screen prospective employees through social network sites. Almost 70 per cent said they had rejected candidates on the basis of what they found there (van Dijck 2013: 212). Readers might reflect on whether, should they never be able to update their Facebook account after today, they would be happy with the summative representation of self it offers. Daniel Trottier refers to the negative effects that information shared on social media sites can have on us – especially with regard to sensitive personal details, or details that later *become* sensitive – as 'digital stigma', noting the extent to which a reputation can be compromised online (2014: 1).

On looking at various social networking sites in particular, we might note that our self-representations are intimately entwined with the self-representations of others. Tweets that use my handle, mention my name, or retweet my posts, all become a part of the story that I construct, and that is constructed about me within that space. This is demonstrated if we look at a high profile example. On 5th March 2014 UK Prime Minister David Cameron tweeted an image purportedly showing him on a direct phoneline to Barack Obama, looking very concerned and more than a little posed. The text read: 'I have been speaking to @BarackObama about the situation in Ukraine. We are united in condemnation of Russia's actions'. The tweet, deemed by many to be a surreal and inappropriate overshare, was extensively parodied online and memes circulated showing increasingly bizarre reconstructions of the image, including eventually by British Shakespearean actor Patrick Stewart. Stewart's tweet read '@David_Cameron @BarackObama I'm now patched in as well. Sorry for the delay', and in the accompanying image Stewart could be seen, po-faced, with a packet of wet wipes held to his ear instead of a phone. The original, which was an attempt by David Cameron to produce and promote a very particular version of self, is imitated here as a part of Patrick Stewart's own construction of self; as somebody with a sense of humour and irony, politically astute, plugged into the playful spirit of social media. Patrick Stewart's re-interpretation of the original tweet then also becomes a part of the story of how David Cameron is represented within the social mediascape; in sum, each has informed the possibilities for self-construction of the other within the Twittersphere.

A similar phenomenon can be found in Facebook, where an individual's self-representation is in part anchored by photos or status updates within which they are tagged, and where their image/name is being used to help others articulate their identities also. Our accounts can also be easily hijacked by others – think for example of the practice of 'fraping'. Other behaviours we might find troubling include trolling and flaming (see also Chapter 2); given the opportunity to self-represent, it is only natural that some people will say things that we do not wish to hear, that offend us, or undo our carefully crafted version of self.

Other opportunities for self-representation might be best understood as marketing activity; companies use our willingness to self-represent as a means of constructing their brand identities also. In a 2015 Budweiser campaign amateur footballers were asked to upload their own #dreamgoal to be shared on the website (Budweiser 2015); social media are often handled very well by big corporations who are able to leverage them to their advantage, and understand the power of a good meme (Shifman 2014).

In all of these sites, we might note, we have very limited information about who the audience is. Anyone can of course potentially view a bit of digital content we produce, but we remain uncertain about who in fact is accessing it (we might have the know how to produce statistics, but they will only tell us so much). So we have to create content for an imagined audience. We choose a language, style, and platform that we think will best fit and speak our identity and take cues from the media environment about how we should act, talk, and refer to ourselves within that context. This imagined community may of course be entirely different from the actual audience (boyd 2007). This question about who is watching links to the larger question of how social media in particular link into surveillance cultures. Daniel Trottier notes in *Social Media and Surveillance* that there are no less than four possibilities for surveillance of our interactions. First, interpersonal surveillance, the surveillance of others which characterizes our every interaction within social media sites like Facebook; 'actively watching and being watched' (Trottier 2012: 30). Second, the scrutiny of whole populations in operation within institutions; whether businesses watching their staff, or universities keeping an eye on their students. Third, market surveillance, and the raft of uses of our data for public relations, customer services and market researchers. And fourth, the value that such information has to agencies who wish to 'police social life' (2012: 31), most notably the police themselves.

In the light of all of those forms of surveillance we might wish to think twice about what we post about ourselves within social media (or allow others to post of course). We might also need to think carefully about who we connect with in such spaces; which one of our 'friends' could be our undoing? Trottier uses the analogy of the wall to question such a culture:

> Walls are supposed to shield from public scrutiny, to ensure dignity and to protect from worst tendencies. In the age of Facebook, walls become a public display of our personal lives.
>
> (Trottier 2012: 4)

It becomes clear that, as Mallan and Giardina recognize, we oscillate between conflicting peril and pleasure concerns as we represent ourselves online (Mallan and Giardina 2009).

THE ANATOMY OF A FACEBOOK PAGE

> How do we 'stage' the life we lead on Facebook? What does one choose to share and with whom? Is Facebook a place for raw emotions or is it a highly stylised presentation of life? What kind of information and emotions are acceptable to share and what is not to be shared on Facebook? And does this vary with age and generations?
>
> (Hilsen and Helvik 2012: 4)

As we have noted, self-representation within the digital mediascape is an act of construction which implicates both the individual who seeks to represent, and the programmes within which those representations are produced. As such, they are a collaborative endeavour and never a straightforward projection of the individual's selfhood. Self-representation is however, as Enli and Thumim note, rarely the main aim as articulated by users of those spaces; their main aim is to socialize and not 'to fulfil a burning desire to represent themselves' (2012: 97). They go on: 'Nevertheless, in order to participate in the *practice* of Facebook, participants must construct self-representations' (Enli and Thumim 2012: 97). A close look at the ways Facebook facilitates particular kinds of self-formation over others through its interface can be enlightening, and bring us closer to an exploration of the questions raised by Hilsen and Helvik above.

On signing up for a profile, a Facebook user agrees to a number of things as part of their Statement of Rights and Responsibilities:

- You will not provide any false personal information on Facebook, or create an account for anyone other than yourself without permission.
- You will not create more than one personal account.
- If we disable your account, you will not create another one without our permission.
- You will not use your personal timeline primarily for your own commercial gain, and will use a Facebook Page for such purposes.
- You will not use Facebook if you are under 13.
- You will not use Facebook if you are a convicted sex offender.
- You will keep your contact information accurate and up-to-date.
- You will not share your password (or in the case of developers, your secret key), let anyone else access your account, or do anything else that might jeopardize the security of your account.
- You will not transfer your account (including any Page or application you administer) to anyone without first getting our written permission. (Facebook 2015)

We have noted that these rules can be stifling for some whose identities are not straightforward or are characterized by plurality. But users work around this, and despite the guidelines, insist on playfulness and raising questions about authenticity with regard to both profile name and profile image: how do we know someone is who they say they are? That their photo is up-to-date? That they exist at all? These questions are not new to social networks, having characterized debate about cybercultures and digital identity since the 1980s (Turkle 1984, 1995, 2011).

In the About section for each profile, a user has an opportunity to add more detailed information about themselves, but along a number of pre-determined trajectories: Work and Education (adding workplaces, schools and colleges); Places You've Lived; Basic Information ('basic' information includes birthdate, gender – which is now customizable, language, religious views, political views); Family and Relationships; Life Events (along a startling array of themes from military service to overcoming an illness); and Further Details About You (including favourite quotes and a number of text boxes). These are worth recounting in depth because they demonstrate how neatly and completely Facebook now compartmentalizes identity and the chronology of a life. Here, users have to fit themselves to the boxes defined as important by Facebook in relation to self. This is for obvious reasons related to the business model of the site; data needs to be harvestable for advertisers, and thus needs to be standardized. This can result in a rather traditional and unimaginative way of conceptualizing identity. The Timeline itself is also an identity management tool which enforces 'a uniform presentation style on all its members' homepages' (van Dijck, 2013: 200); a narrative biography, chronicling your life. To van Dijck, 'All online lives contain the same key ingredients' (van Dijck 2013: 205).

Other mechanisms through which users self-identify in Facebook are through the additional opportunities to add sports, music, TV programmes, films, books, apps and games, and the Like function which allows users to demonstrate allegiance along a staggering range of trajectories; from restaurants and arts institutions, to people, events and news outlets. What we 'Like' within Facebook tells other users something else about the self we are constructing within that space; our affiliative identity. But there are some pretty quirky findings emerging about Facebook Likes and what they can tell us:

> For example, the best predictors of high intelligence include "Thunderstorms," "The Colbert Report," "Science," and "Curly Fries," whereas low intelligence was indicated by "Sephora," "I Love Being A Mom," "Harley Davidson," and "Lady Antebellum." Good predictors of male homosexuality included "No H8 Campaign," "Mac Cosmetics," and "Wicked The Musical," whereas strong predictors of male heterosexuality included "Wu-Tang Clan," "Shaq," and "Being Confused

> After Waking Up From Naps." Although some of the Likes clearly relate to their predicted attribute, as in the case of No H8 Campaign and homosexuality, other pairs are more elusive; there is no obvious connection between Curly Fries and high intelligence.
>
> (Kosinki et al. 2013: 5804)

Such predictors are of course a valuable way of building user profiles, and targeting advertising more effectively. Within Facebook we are never far away from corporate interests through advertising, but also in the form of Likes; often referencing consumer and retail brands. In Facebook, the link between self-representation and the critique of neoliberalism is perhaps most starkly confronted.

An inclusive notion of 'friendship' is at the heart of the Facebook business model centred on monetizing weak ties between individuals. The status update tool allows us to communicate our every move to those friends, and to engage in a dialogue with them in response. As Trottier notes, 'To "friend" another user means more than acknowledging that you know – or want to know – them. Friending also involves sharing personal information with that person' (2012: 3). Within our timeline, we can of course add all kinds of multimedia presentations of self including photos, audio, maps and video. They all come together to construct a version of self that is in dialogue with the self-constructions of others; those others might, for example, tag me in a photo they have uploaded, or draw attention to an article I might like using my name. As Enli and Thumim note, 'on Facebook, other people are simultaneously representing you as part of their own self-representations' (2012: 100). That is much easier now Facebook uses facial recognition softwares. I am the editor of the content on my page, but the editors of the content on my wall are the friends who decide to Like and Comment, and to Share. On occasion this can lead to forms of self-spectacle (to extend Debord 1967); suddenly being presented with a view of self that you were not expecting and may even feel uncomfortable with, a kind of voyeurism of self.

The selves we create in Facebook operate at the nexus of online and offline. Using Facebook is a part of many individuals' daily social lives, but it has also become a way of enabling them to organize their social lives in the offline world. The principle defining logic of Facebook, beyond the concept of Friending, is one of openness. Openness if a default setting in Facebook, with Privacy settings being the best example. Privacy has become one of the most controversial of topics with regard to Facebook, and in many ways we are seeing a collapse in the dichotomy between public and private practices of self-construction. Some users navigate this better than others of course, being very strategic about who sees particular bits of content, and who does not. As Trottier notes, one has to 'maintain a vigilant familiarity' with privacy settings which are often revised and modified without our knowledge (Trottier 2014: 2)

When we log into Facebook and look at our wall, what we see is an amalgamation of atoms of content posted by ourselves, our friends, their friends, companies and organizations that we like, or those our friends may like. The wall is not neutral. It is not a blank slate upon which we write ourselves. Rather, it is underpinned by one of the most complex filtering algorithms in the world, one that looks at more than a thousand data signals before deciding what to show us (Madrigal 2015). As such, Facebook is entirely responsible for crafting our social experiences of that network. In 2014 Facebook was in the papers for carrying out what was called a 'mood experiment'; trying to manipulate the mood of 689,000 users by filtering only certain kinds of content their way in a bid to explore 'emotional contagion' (Kramer et al. 2014). In such circumstances, we begin to see that not only are we not as in control of our self-representations as we might like to think within Facebook, but that our very psychological state is up for grabs also.

ASSESSING THE CLAIMS MADE ABOUT SELF-REPRESENTATION AND ITS CONSEQUENCES

There have been many claims made for the benefits of self-representation. First, and perhaps most problematically is the claim that increased opportunities for self-representation will re-balance power relations both within the media and in society. That self-representation will free us from the shackles of 'big media' is of course a problematic assertion, and not one that is borne out by the evidence to date. Apart from anything else, we are still very much reliant on gatekeepers to our media, even if those gatekeepers change over time; Facebook, LinkedIn, YouTube. As such, any claim that self-representations are unmediated is also a spurious one. A site such as YouTube is a good example here, it is very much mediated. In YouTube we don't see realities, but people's version of realities as played out through the tools they have at their disposal. We see conscious decisions about editing, selection, remixing, framing and music. People use increasingly sophisticated softwares with filters and in-built music choices, such as the raft of stop motion movie applications. YouTube films are not 'the truth' any more than the representations discussed in other chapters.

Second is the claim that opportunities for self-representation necessarily multiply the range of representations on offer; that within the Twittersphere, or YouTube for example, there are more diverse and layered identities displayed, and we have the chance to broaden our experiential horizons. As a result, it is hoped, we will learn more about other cultures than we might otherwise: we can satisfy our curiosity by watching clips on YouTube that are not filtered through the lense of mainstream media; we can learn more about those whose political leanings differ from our own; we can access content from around the globe and move between contexts quite seamlessly. As a consequence, we are perhaps liberated to imagine ourselves differently, or to 'read' those other to ourselves in more nuanced ways. Again the evidence on this is somewhat disheartening, showing that in actual fact, in the online space, we refer to a very limited range of sources, use limited search terms, and seek out content that reflects rather than challenges our world views (Hindman 2009). Just think for a moment about those you follow on Twitter. They are likely to be those with interests akin to your own, or who represent something you aspire to. As such, our realms of experience online do not differ wildly from those we operate within offline. An associated claim is that we have the capacity to present multilayered versions of self or even adopt contrary identity attachments given the opportunity for anonymity afforded in much online communication. Yet we should be reminded that within Facebook, it remains a breach of the end-user agreement to use any name other than a 'real-name', or to have multiple accounts. This courted negative publicity in 2014 when it emerged that drag artists who were not using their legal names were having their accounts deactivated by the company. This was seen as a shortsighted and even bigoted move, as Holpuch noted 'Thousands rallied around the queens and others who might choose to use an alias on Facebook for safety reasons, like domestic abuse survivors or activists' (Holpuch 2014). A similar concern was at the heart of a recent crackdown in China on the use of pseudonyms and the setting up of parody accounts. This 'vulgar culture' as it was termed by the Cyberspace Administration of China was seen as symptomatic of a trend toward illegal and unhealthy internet usage that subverted state power (BBC News 2015b).

Third is the claim that self-representations open up the public discourse because anybody can make them. It might be true that the technology is increasingly intuitive and the barriers to entry get lower all of the time (if you have the requisite digital literacy) and that as a result the boundaries between production and consumption become blurred, but it remains the case that not everybody can take up that opportunity. A 2009 study of Twitter found that 10 per cent of Twitter users generate 90 per cent of the content (Heil and Piskorski 2009). This has been called the 1 per cent rule; most people on Twitter have only tweeted once. We have noted already the persistence of a substantial digital divide; one that replicates real world inequalities and prejudices within the online environment (Taylor 2014). Those who are disenfranchised offline remain so online (Hindman 2009). One final claim that we might question is the assertion that the distribution of such self-representations is so straightforward and dematerialized that audiences for output will be global. There is of course nothing inevitable about that. We might note the increased capacity to speak and to self-represent, but who indeed is listening? Who, if anyone, is watching?

In the next chapter we extend this discussion with a look at the kinds of representations of self on offer within the reality TV genre.

NOTES

1 Web 1.0 in contrast – describing websites in the 1990s – was characterized by static pages, and a straightforwardly broadcast model of communications (Gere 2008; O'Reilly 2005).

2 An emergent term that can be credited to Adi Kuntsman, Farida Vis and Simon Faulkner, organizers of the 'Selfie Citizenship' workshop at Manchester Metropolitan University, April 2015 https://sites.google.com/site/selfiecitizenship/home, accessed 27th March 2015.

4

REALITY TV

Reality TV is one of the sites where our uneasiness about representation is most graphically manifested. The study of this genre
picks up on many of the themes detailed in the other chapters of
this book, not least our analyses of self-representation and the
construction of 'reality' through media texts. This chapter will
review definitions of reality TV, noting their fluidity, and the
increasing integration of the form with discourses about surveillance, celebrity and the consumer society. One recurring theme
will be the variety of ethical considerations that are inevitably at
the core of both the production and study of reality television,
and I introduce those here with a brief example.

The name and face of Reeva Steenkamp were widely featured
in international news reporting in 2013 when she was shot dead
by her partner Oscar Pistorius at his home in Pretoria, South
Africa, on Valentine's Day. Steenkamp was a model who had only
recently signed up to, and begun filming, the reality TV series
Tropika Island of Treasure before her death. She only became a
'star' of reality television posthumously. At the time of her death
there was some discussion about the ethics of airing the episodes

of the series that she had appeared in. Would it be a 'fitting tribute' to Reeva, as the producers of the show argued? Or would it be interpreted as the programme makers cashing in on her death; a purely commercial decision to transmit? It was reported that the television network was charging $3,000 for short clips from the series to use in news reporting of her death (Reilly 2013). People wanted to see not only still images of Steenkamp, but her moving, talking, 'authentic' self on screen. Much was made of an exit interview she had filmed wherein she commented, 'I think that the way you go out, not just your journey in life but the way that you go out and you make your exit is so important' (Reilly 2013). This was framed within reporting as a prophetic utterance, all the more profound due to the fact of its being a presentation of self. Australian reporters called it a 'haunting TV show message' as if it had been left with intent from beyond the grave (news. com.au 2013) Footage of her swimming with dolphins on the show was widely distributed, demonstrating her reported innocence, kindness and vibrancy, and its repetition nodded to the scale of the tragedy that had befallen her. We see in this example how the performance of self within the television programme became a shorthand for telling us about who Steenkamp was in actuality, and how little control she (and her family perhaps) eventually had over its circulation. In reality TV, there are questions about the ethics of representation that loom large, as we will see.

But we can extend our discussion of reality TV with reference to this case, for the ensuing trial of Oscar Pistorius, and the media attention that it courted, had all of the makings of a courtroom reality show in its own right. Pistorius, the mythologized 'blade runner', the 'superhuman', the 'sci-fi athlete' (Lewis 2014) went on trial for murder in March 2014, and it was not until six months later, in September that year, that he was finally found guilty of culpable homicide. It was another month before Pistorius was sentenced to five years in prison.[1] As TIME Magazine stated on its dedicated cover spread at the time, Pistorius' dominant interpretive frame had changed from 'Man' to 'Superman', and finally to 'Gunman' (TIME 2013).

What made the case so spectacular was not only its incredibly high profile protagonist, but the decision to broadcast the trial on radio and television. South Africa's Eyewitness News launched a pop-up radio station, rolling news channels aired the coverage, reporters from all over the world presented daily news packages using footage from the courtroom (see Figure 4.1), and a raft of documentaries were produced. Reporters Joseph and Blignaut, for South Africa's City Press, noted at the time that the trial was 'like a new breed of reality TV', with 'uncanny parallels to the OJ Simpson trial' (2014). They reasoned the appeal of the trial was due to the very high stakes at play; life and death, incarceration and freedom, and the irresistible 'fall from grace' of Pistorius, a man simultaneously both vulnerable and strong (Joseph and Blignaut 2014). The daily reporting was not unlike the rolling narrative of the reality television show (in the vein of Big Brother); full of drama, conflict, and intensely personal. Pistorius, central to the drama, was unable to step outside of it and give us his reflections, being trapped within the world that was the courtroom. Within various social media platforms there was live reporting of the hearing, and of course much discussion. As with many reality TV formats judging was a trope being played out; there was obviously somebody sitting in judgement within the courtroom, but we too sat in judgement in our living rooms and in front of our screens. The footage from the court raised questions that are pertinent to a broader analysis of reality TV; how

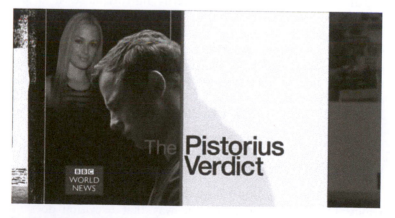

Figure 4.1 Pistorius Verdict BBC News 24 Special, BBC

was it being edited and staged? Where was the boundary between public and private, and how was it being demarcated (if at all)? Who was being exploited; Steenkamp's family perhaps, or Pistorius himself? What was happening to Pistorius' celebrity, and were we comfortable with that? As with much other reality TV output, the trial became the centre of media attention, and in another similarity, it sparked discussion about wider cultural issues; in this case the high murder rate in South Africa, violent crime against women, the experience of disability, and the robustness of the South African legal system itself.

A look at this example not only alerts us to some of the issues that are at stake in the study of reality TV representations, including ethical ones, but alerts us to the fact that, as Hill says, reality TV is 'a genre in transition' (Hill 2005: 41) and one difficult to define. There are many questions we should ask about reality TV as a representational medium including: How does the presence of a camera modify behaviours and the performance of self? In what ways might reality TV be said to be an authentic version of reality? What do the 'casting' processes associated with reality TV suggest? How might the 'value' of reality TV be discerned (and why do we insist on debating the 'value' of this particular genre over others)? Is it democratic and serving of a civic purpose, or is it voyeuristic and cheap exploitation? How do localized versions of global franchises reflect local concerns and discourses if at all? And lastly, how does reality TV link into discourses about our wider cultures of surveillance? These are questions that I begin to explore in this chapter, pointing readers to a raft of exceptionally good analyses of reality TV which can provide more comprehensive and in-depth overviews of the production, reception and societal significance of reality TV than I am able to do here (Hill 2005, 2015, Deery 2015, Kavka 2012, Holmes and Jermyn 2004, McGrath 2004).

WHAT IS REALITY TV?

As Misha Kavka asserts below there can be no doubting that reality TV has ably disrupted the way that television does its business (Deery 2015):

One cannot overestimate the impact of reality TV. In just two decades, it has transformed programming schedules, branded satellite and digital channels, created a celebrity industry in its own right and turned viewers into savvy readers of – not to mention potential participant in – the mechanics of television production.

(Kavka 2012: 2)

According to Murray and Ouellette, its influence has been profound within media and cultural studies scholarship also, altering the very direction of television studies itself (2009: 3). Reality TV is a genre with a conflicted relationship with audiences; one they will simultaneously deny watching, yet register high levels of enjoyment for (Riddle and De Simone 2013). In 2015 reality TV is a global phenomenon. The *X Factor* for example has had franchises in no fewer than 40 countries including China, Colombia, the Czech Republic, Chile, India, Israel, Australia, New Zealand, the United Kingdom, Russia, the United States and Vietnam, and those countries invariably have their own homegrown series within that landscape as well. A definition of reality TV is however not easy to pin down, particularly in terms of the inclusion and exclusion of sub-genres. It is clear that the 'reality' claims of the title are problematic, but we might consider the 'TV' referent to be increasingly so also.

Misha Kavka introduces her book on the subject by noting that 'If there is a simple definition of reality television then we might say that the term refers to unscripted shows with nonprofessional actors being observed by cameras in preconfigured environments' (Kavka 2012: 5). Annette Hill notes that 'reality TV is a catch-all category that includes a wide range of entertainment programmes about real people... reality TV is located in border territories, between information and entertainment, documentary and drama' (Hill 2005: 2). So, reality TV is actuality-based; factual, unscripted, about 'real' people being observed by cameras, and by extension, viewers. It has been called 'popular factual programming' (Corner 2000: 687), and it certainly is popular with audiences, and as a consequence, with programme producers and television executives also. A look at the viewing figures in any of the countries identified above confirms that 'the reality genre has mass appeal' (Hill 2005: 2). For example, in the United States Nielsen reported four reality shows in the top 10 primetime television broadcasts of 2013; *Dancing with the Stars* and its results show, and the two separate weekly broadcasts of *American Idol*. Each separate broadcast was averaging approximately 13 to 14 million viewers (Nielsen 2013). Interestingly, in their first reporting of registered Twitter activity before, during and after shows, Nielsen also noted that *Dancing with the Stars* was averaging 78,000 tweets per show, whilst both *X Factor* and *The Voice* were averaging more than 200,000 tweets per show (Nielsen 2013). These figures are significant: big audiences of course lead to bigger financial gains in terms of advertising revenues. Lest we forget, reality TV is 'an unabashedly commercial genre' (Murray and Ouellette 2009: 3). Such programmes also attract audiences that are seen as particularly appealing to advertisers, namely that allusive hard to reach younger adult audience. Murray and Ouellette suggest that it is precisely this popularity coupled with the embrace of commercialism that differentiates reality TV from (say) news or documentary which also make 'truth claims' but fulfill peoples expectations about 'serious' programming as being both unpopular and unprofitable (2009: 4).

The figures look even better when you consider how cheap reality TV can be to make. According to Annette Hill writing in 2005, there were fewer crew members, fewer scriptwriters, and at that time no professional – unionized – actors, making it a veritable, and saleable, goldmine of a format. The rise of reality TV was well-timed in this regard. In the 1990s and of course into the 2000s, the economic context within which the cultural industries operated meant that 'networks were looking for a quick fix solution', and so we witnessed the rise – and rise – of reality TV, accompanied by an increase in tabloid journalism (Hill 2005). Glynn has even posited that reality TV might be understood as itself a form of 'tabloid television' (Glynn 2000).

According to Misha Kavka (2012), the history of reality TV can be broken down into three 'generations' of content featuring different typologies of programming and broadly aligned to time periods. For Kavka the first generation roughly coincides with the 1990s (1989–99) and might be understood as the camcorder generation of programmes like *America's Most Wanted* (US 1988[2]) and *Cops* (US 1989); pursuit and its consequences were core to the genre at that time. *America's Most Wanted* was made locally (by state), and with a view to performing a civic service; assisting those in law enforcement to apprehend those on the run from the law. Interestingly, given our previous discussion about the Pistorius trial, we might note that the now infamous police pursuit of American footballer OJ Simpson happened in 1994, right in the middle of this time period. The pursuit was filmed by an LA News Service helicopter and live broadcast on the news in a mirroring of what was happening on reality television (you can still view that footage online). This was also the period of the docu-soap; in the UK *The Cruise* (1997), *Driving School* (1997) and *Airport* (1996) for example all became talking points, and a number of 'characters' featured within them became household names, some for significant periods. Jane McDonald from *The Cruise* and Jeremy Spake from *Airport* for example went on to achieve notoriety at that time. We started to see the attachment of celebrity, and its transferal into other programme genres and media output. This was most bizarrely exemplified when Maureen Rees, a Welsh cleaner from *Driving School* released a cover of Madness' 'Driving In My Car' which actually entered the UK singles charts (although not very spectacularly).

According to Kavka, the second generation of reality TV (from 1999 to 2005) saw the rise of the competition format; pitting one 'contestant' against another, and often including a vote or final judgement as a climactic – and often participatory – element in the show. High profile examples such as *Big Brother* (Netherlands 1999), *The Apprentice* (US 2004) and *The Bachelor* (US 2002) exemplified this shift, and raised many ethical questions for programme makers and audiences alike about surveillance, casting, exploitation and the spectacle (we will come onto these in turn). This period also saw a diversification of media platforms for the delivery of content; for the first time channels had web micro-sites for additional information, footage and (eventually) discussion. We could now watch the participant-contestants in *Big Brother* 24 hours a day, and 'immediacy and authenticity' were the new promise of the form (Kavka 2012: 85).

Kavka's third generation of reality TV overlaps the second, beginning around 2002 and running to this day. This is a generation of programmes that are concerned with the production and maintenance of celebrity. So, you get the rise of the talent show format (*Got Talent* [US 2006], *The Voice* [the Netherlands 2010], *Top Model* [US 2003]), the 'no talent required' format, which takes celebrities that are often produced by reality TV shows themselves and follows their daily movements (*Keeping Up with the Kardashians* [US 2007], *What Katie Did Next* [UK 2009]), and lastly, the 'celebrity maintenance' format (*Dancing with the Stars* [US 2005], *Celebrity Big Brother* [UK 2001], *I'm a Celebrity… Get Me Out of Here!* [UK 2002]) which makes plain the constructive nature of celebrity (or 'celebritisation', Thompson et al. 2014) and the commodification of self, but also highlights the transience of celebrity within the wider ecology of the media. This is a really interesting development as 'reality TV disengages from its documentary roots and becomes a self-conscious participant in the rituals of self-commodification and self-legitimation that define contemporary celebrity culture' (Kavka 2012: 9–10). In 2013, Chinese reality TV show *Where Are We Going Dad?* took this format to a new extreme of popularity. As five celebrity dads and their children went on excursions and took part in tasks, 600 million Chinese tuned in every week. Before the series had finished its first season, it was reported that celebrities were 'clamoring' to take part in the second season (Jin 2013).

Within these formats reality stars such as Kim Kardashian and Katie Price 'have afforded viewers unprecedented access into their lives' and are part of 'a growing subgenre of reality TV [which] simply allows audiences to watch people do nothing more than run errands, eat meals, take vacations, plan parties, argue, and fall in and out of love' (Riddle and De Simone 2013: 237). Such characters have been integral to the ongoing critique of capitalist consumerism and its presentation as aspirational and desirable (Thompson et al. 2014), and it has been posited that within reality TV platforms, the distinction between self and consumption becomes blurred in practices of self-branding; people become 'image-entrepreneurs' (Hearn 2008: 208), savvy to the (potentially) multiple benefits of self-commodification.

In 2015 we might wish to add a fourth generation of reality TV as an extension to that narrative: the structured reality format (often also termed scripted or mixed reality). Given the extent to which, in its own right, it has extended the debate about reality TV, its definition, and its relationship with celebrity, this format seems more than worthy of note. This format emerged in the United States from 2006 with *The Hills* and later *Jersey Shore* (2009), and in the United Kingdom with programmes like *Geordie Shore* (2011), *The Only Way Is Essex* (2010), and *Made in Chelsea* (2011). The term structured reality 'best reflects the form's blending of fictional storytelling with reality TV (Khalsa 2011, 34; Raeside 2011, 6)' (Woods 2012: 2), and knowingly nods to the reworking of the reality TV format for audiences raised on celebrity gossip magazines and *Big Brother*. In such examples, we might be seeing a new brand of celebrity; what Grindstaff and Murray call 'more "ordinary" forms of celebrity' (2015: 109)

The Only Way Is Essex (TOWIE), perhaps the best known example of the format in the UK at least, was first aired in 2010 and continues to be made by ITV, the UK's longest established commercial television network. As I write in March 2015 it is airing its fourteenth series. TOWIE was an immediate hit with audiences, although television critics seemed unsure what to make of it, caught up in a pre-occupation with its relationship to the 'real'. The programme, narrated by well-known Essex personality Denise Van-Outen, kick-started Series 1 Episode 1 with the following announcement:

> This Programme contains flash cars, big watches and false boobs. The tans you see might be fake but the people are all real although some of what they do has been set up purely for your entertainment.
>
> (Series 1, Episode 1)

In 2015 that unabashed and tongue-in-cheek articulation has changed very little:

> This programme contains cute puppies, old grudges and some serious sweet-talking. Some of the pearly whites you see may be fake but these people are all real, although some of what they do has been given a rocking remix for your entertainment.
>
> (Series 14, Episode 10)

Figure 4.2 The Only Way Is Essex, ITV

The programme makers have found a way of articulating structured reality that clearly sits ok with its audiences or at least does not alienate them. This prelude is honest and opaque in equal measure, the extent of the series' construction remaining allusive. Such is the structured reality format; non-professional actors placed in structured scenarios or 'pseudo-environments', which elicit certain kinds of (perhaps predictable) action and conversation (Thompson et al. 2014: 480). 'Story producers' storyboard what they are going to film in advance after discussion with the cast, priming their subjects to discuss certain topics, with an outcome in mind, although they cannot always predict that outcome (Raeside 2011). Structured reality is very playful, and, according to Faye Woods, 'offers a skeptical viewing position and knowing address that allows viewers to be detached yet simultaneously invested in the unfolding narratives' (Woods 2012: 2). As such, it recognizes its own 'artificiality' (ibid.). We might note that contrary to popular belief this *can* make for a very sophisticated interpretive experience. TOWIE's viewers spoke in their thousands in 2011, voting for the programme to win the Audience Award at the 2011 British Academy Film and Television Arts award (a BAFTA); the highest profile – and most prestigious – television awards in the country. This was a vote that surprised both the cast, and the 'great and good' of the entertainment establishment. Some of their fellow nominees, including the makers and casts of *Downton Abbey* and *Sherlock* could hardly hide their disdain. *The Guardian* reported:

> the actor's expression spoke volumes about the television establishment's reaction to a bunch of spray-tanned amateurs waltzing off with a trophy more usually afforded to skilled craftspeople... The Only Way is Essex has replaced Big Brother as the programme people sneer about at dinner parties without having seen it.
>
> (Raeside 2011)

It is too easy to dismiss out of hand the popularity of – and public adoration for – the 'casts' of such programmes (and 'casts' they are), and the associations with fame that go with them. As Kavka noted in 2012 of reality TV more broadly:

> [even though] popular discourse readily associates reality television with fame, it does so in a negative way, dismissing reality TV participants as fame-mongers, 'wannabes' and untalented nobodies looking for their fifteen minutes in the limelight. In the rare cases when reality TV alumni manage to stretch their provisional fame into greater media visibility, they tend to be derided as 'D-list' celebrities who will do anything for attention.
>
> (Kavka 2012: 145)

This has been no more the case than with the structured reality sub-genre, which has also re-ignited the debate about whether reality TV constitutes a genre in its own right. To this day, books published on the topic of reality TV often have a chapter dedicated to this question. Annette Hill asserts that reality TV brings together 'a range of formats with distinctive programme characteristics' (Hill 2005: 8). According to Hill in 2005, formats included talent formats, celebrity formats, infotainment, life experiment formats, docusoap and reality games. We might now add structured reality also. If reality TV is one genre, it is one with many sub-genres that are evolving all of the time and do not remain static. Indeed some programmes still defy classification. *Storage Wars* for example (US 2010), an American reality show which sees participants bidding to buy the contents of storage containers, is a difficult one to classify. It is competitive, but hardly a talent show or a straightforward gaming format. *Storage Wars* also demonstrates that it can be difficult to predict what will be a hit and what will be a miss in this area. We see new and hybrid genres emerging all of the time – the scripted reality format itself is a hybrid genre, and we might also note the parody reality format as exemplified in *The Office* (UK 2001, then US 2005) or *Modern Family* (US 2009). These series, often called mockumentaries, mimic the aesthetic of reality TV and feed off discourses around self-representation, exploitation and surveillance, raising questions about where documentary meets reality TV. As Annette Hill notes, 'formats for reality TV... quickly become yesterday's news' (Hill 2005: 38); 'television often cannibalises itself, feeding off successful genre and formats in order to create new hybrid programmes' (Hill 2005: 42).

Thus we see how the genre has changed over the years, and might begin to question how useful the recourse to 'reality' is in the face of scrutiny. Perhaps at its worst it misleads audiences, oversimplifying the connection and divesting them of responsibility to think about the ethics of the format, and at its best limits the potentials of programme makers to push at the boundaries of the form, or to do things differently. This will be unpacked in the next section.

THE 'REAL' IN REALITY TV

Reality TV formats have multiplied to the point that they have become self-conscious parodies of their original premise of access to the unscripted interactions of people who are not professional entertainers. The genre has done little to follow through on the promise to 'share' control with viewers by setting aside hackneyed formulas. Rather, reality shows are becoming the latest and most self-conscious in a string of transparently staged spectacles, complete with their own formulas and increasingly reliant on a cast of demicelebrities culled from the pool of would-be actors who do the rounds of the reality TV casting calls on the advice of their agents.

(Andrejevic 2004: 3)

It is clearly too simplistic to assert that reality TV mirrors, or even approximates, 'the real' (Couldry 2006). It has been noted throughout this book how tricky the relationship between 'reality' and 'representation' is, re-iterating time and again that representations are constructs that in themselves help to create our social world. Andrejevic's searing commentary above references this, but reminds us that with regard to reality TV this relationship is particularly problematic because of the truth claims that have been made on behalf of the genre. These are especially apparent if you look at the inception of formats such as *Big Brother* which were promoted very much as social experiments, and not as socialized performances. Brenton and Cohen recount the origins of *Big Brother* in 'Biosphere-type seclusion' and self-sufficiency (2003: 60). This is clearly a long way from the *Celebrity Big Brother* format that has proven to be so popular (UK 2001).

This question is one that has vexed many scholars and critics, as we began to see in our discussion of structured reality television above. To quote a few scholars on this matter:

> The debate about what is real and what is not is the million-dollar question for popular factual television.
>
> (Hill 2005: 57)

> one of the most recurrent features of the popular and critical reception of reality TV has been comment on the ways in which it manipulates and constructs 'the real', and hence the contested nature of the term 'Reality TV' itself.
>
> (Holmes and Jermyn 2004: 11)

As we have noted, these questions are now open to intense scrutiny by audiences themselves who, rather than accepting reality TV simply *as* reality, tend to be involved in ongoing and searching analyses of the texts themselves as they watch. To return to *Big Brother* again in order to exemplify, it has become the norm for audiences to make accusations that contestants are playing up for the cameras or too 'aware' of their presence, to charge them with game playing and to question their motivations for taking part; only being in it for the celebrity for example. These themes are also of course a topic of debate amongst participants in the programmes themselves who are often incredibly pre-occupied with how they may be being represented and perceived 'on the outside'; As Holmes and Jermyn note, 'it is now routine ... for participants to talk explicitly about the politics of how they are being "represented" at the level of the *text itself*' (Holmes and Jermyn 2004: 12). For Annette Hill, the concepts of 'authenticity' and 'performance' are often invoked to give us a way into this debate: but both are problematic (Hill 2005) there being an ongoing trade-off between the two. We might *crave* authenticity in reality TV; but we *expect* performances of all kinds:

> There are emotional, physical and vocal performances, judging performance skills, and the performance of people participating in the show as themselves, as contestants and as live crowds and audiences.
>
> (Hill 2015)

'Verisimilitude' can be a useful concept here, a way of talking about the extent to which a text resembles 'reality'. As we have noted, all texts are constructs, and none can be straightforwardly understood as real, but some texts are of course more believable than others. To stray into the historical film genre for a moment to exemplify, we might note that *Schindler's List* (1993) has a high degree of verisimilitude; being in black and white it is easy to believe it's 'truth', making it akin to archival footage, and placing it as very much a narrative grounded in a past that can be known. *Big Brother* was conceived to have a high degree of cultural verisimilitude; to reference and replicate the norms of our everyday social world and to open them up for observation within the world created on screen. But we might note that over time audiences have been critical of the extent to which that can be said to be the case. We might now talk about other forms of reality TV as having more verisimilitude than Big Brother, *Gogglebox* for example (2013, referenced below) is, on the face of it at least, almost *too* real; too close to our own realities as we watch the watchers, and could to all intents and purposes *be* the watchers on screen. Yet we are reminded that these are performances of self we witness on the various stages of reality TV.

This brings us back to Goffman's theory of the presentation of self introduced in the previous chapter. Reality TV in the form of the first series of *Big Brother*, was premised on the idea that we might get beyond the 'frontstage' presentation or construction of self, and gain access to those other elements of personality that only emerge over time, and as people's guards are let down. This is still the hope that we entertain as we watch a series like *Big Brother*; we 'search for moments of authenticity when real people are really themselves in a constructed environment' (Woods 2012: 4). This is seldom the case however, as Hill notes, performers act out, 'producing meta versions of themselves they assume producers and audiences want to see' (Hill 2015).

So if we are to conclude that the reality presented within various reality TV formats is frustrated, what might that mean for our analysis of other media as set up in distinction? We have to be careful here. By setting reality TV up as 'unreal' do we present other TV formats or genres such as documentary, or news even, as 'real'? This would be problematic in the extreme, such programming might similarly be accused of manipulation, casting and selective editing and the 'stars' charged with presenting an overblown performance of self; think for example of reporters or politicians on the news, or those filmed for a documentary. Being in front of a camera is not a natural state for most people, and many in the public eye now undergo training to ensure that their performances of self are at best unremarkable in such formats. As Holmes and Jermyn note, there have 'never been any easy distinctions between "drama" and "reality"' (Holmes and Jermyn 2004: 11).

We might also note the capacity that being watched has to validate us, to reassure us that we exist (Biressi and Nunn 2005: 102). This connects with the surveillance cultures we now occupy in most public spaces and areas of our social lives (including of course online as we noted in Chapter 3). Andrejevic notes that with the advent of reality TV, 'Surveillance had itself become a mediated spectacle' (Andrejevic 2004: 2), and Murray and Ouellette note the more sinister extension of this argument, that reality TV might in itself make us more accustomed to being watched, and more relaxed about the consequences of being observed:

> what reality TV teaches us in the early years of the new millennium is that in order to be good citizens we must allow ourselves to be watched as we watch ourselves and those around us, and then modify our conduct and behaviour accordingly.
>
> (Murray and Ouellette 2009: 9)

These links have been troubling to many critics of reality TV, who have questioned the real world ramifications of the acceptance of creeping surveillance in the name of entertainment. Riddle and De Simone speculate that consumption of reality TV might make audiences more prone to sharing their innermost thoughts and emotions via social networks and video sharing sites for example (2013: 237). Daniel Trottier found in a study of social media that some younger respondents drew parallels between what they were doing within social media, and the publicity that reality TV stars actively court (2012: 73). One of his respondents, Rachel, says:

> It's almost as if we're in a world where we watch a lot of reality TV and there's TV shows like *The Hills* and things like that, Facebook is our own little form of entertainment where we can get a glimpse of everyone's life.
>
> (Rachel in Trottier 2012: 73)

It might not be absurd then to conclude that reality TV is at least impacting our attitudes toward surveillance in the twenty-first century, and our desire to be able to 'glimpse' the lives of others often from afar. Surveillance culture is seen as being troubling for a variety of reasons, but of concern to us here is how surveillance culture intersects with our capacity and propensity to self-represent, and whether and how those representations are used by governments, corporations, police and criminals, but also how they might be used by those who are closer to us, our friends, exes or bosses for example (see also Chapter 3).

Such concerns as played out in the debate about reality TV have spawned a range of media texts such as *Ed TV* (1999), *The Truman Show* (1998), even the *Hunger Games* (books published from 2008, and films released from 2012) that seek to work through some of these issues, and follow them to a range of conclusions. In the *Hunger Games*, the upshot of that culture is public gaming for life itself, the winner being the last contestant standing in a televised death match. In the UK, there was also Charlie Brooker's critically acclaimed series *Dead Set* (2008) which explored similar dystopian extensions of the genre. The reality TV show is thus a site of intrigue, fascination and ongoing concern. It is a moving target, in favour one moment and out the next.

One reality TV programme very much in favour in the United Kingdom in 2015 allows us to reflect further on this issue of surveillance: *Gogglebox*. McNulty introduces it thus:

> On paper, with its jokey-title and late-night slot, Gogglebox, which started in April this year, sounded like a final scraping of the reality TV barrel – the moment when TV had finally eaten itself. But from the first episode, it proved to be a hit, enchanting viewers with its portrayal of everyday life and relationships, entertaining us with a fantastic set of real-life characters.
>
> (McNulty 2013)

In this programme viewers watch on as the 'stars', themselves viewers, sit on the sofas in their living rooms and watch television, providing a running – highly opinionated and self-conscious – commentary on the content they are consuming. This is surveillance on an intriguing level, we enter these private, domestic spaces and observe as they observe; an inverse surveillance, we watch the watchers. Our status as voyeur, like their status as voyeur, is destabilized by its relationship with the wider systems of surveillance within which they, and we, participate. Yet we might interpret this as – seemingly at least – a benign and inconsequential surveillance, an opportunity to observe people in their natural habitat; recumbent on the sofa with their feet up and a glass of wine. This is perhaps as close to the promise of the original *Big Brother* as we are likely to get.

Except if we dig a little deeper we again come across the fact that the programme has a frustrated relationship with the real. The participants are of course chosen through a casting process, and some of them have appeared in other reality TV shows. It looks like each of the groups is filmed via a discrete camera in the vicinity of their television, but it is actually two remote cameras, and a

Figure 4.3 Gogglebox, Channel 4

four-person crew sits in the next room watching, giving occasional prompts if the viewers forget that they are supposed to be commentating. So what kind of a reality is this? This is not how the average person or family watches television. Theirs is in actual fact a more challenging performance of self than we might at first have realized. As a viewer it is quite possible to find yourself ruminating that the way you watch television is itself deficient; you are rarely as vocal or as witty as the stars of the show in your own responses to the programmes you watch. But to take up that challenge *without* the cameras rolling makes you feel self-conscious in the extreme and is incredibly challenging; just give it a go. This is a performance of self that is virtually impossible to re-create without surveillance.

THE POLITICS OF REPRESENTATION IN REALITY TV

It has been noted throughout this book that the study of representation is concerned with the politics of gender, sexuality, race, disability, age, class and other social aspects of the individual. Reality TV is often seen as a site of interest and exploration in this debate. Literature both supports and complicates the idea that reality TV can lead to a widening or diversification of televisual representations (Murray and Ouellette 2009).

As we've noted, there is often a rather sneering attitude toward reality TV, its 'stars' and its audiences. It is deemed to be a dumbed-down format 'with a low entry threshold for participants' (Kavka 2012: 145), occupying a space of 'low cultural value' (ibid.). Many of those who have made a name for themselves via the reality TV route (perhaps especially in that third generation of formats, Kavka 2012) are seen as being in some way illegitimate presences within the public domain. They may be on their way to securing financial capital, but they have not secured what Pierre Bourdieu would have called the cultural capital (the non-financial assets: education, intelligence, speech, style, taste) to garner respect (Bourdieu 1986). This attitudinal stance is perhaps best exemplified in the UK if we take a look at the treatment of the new breed of 'celebrity chavs' within the media: Kerry Katona (coined 'pramface' in the press), Jade Goody (called a 'minger' and a 'pig' by the tabloids) and of course the notorious Katie Price (Tyler and Bennett 2010, Woods 2012). We might also bracket the entire cast of *TOWIE* here (both men and women).

Class is regionally coded and very present within much current reality TV output; in *TOWIE* and *Made in Chelsea*, but look also at *Desperate Scousewives* (Liverpool, England 2011) and *The Valleys* (Cardiff, Wales 2012). Here, we see it signified in the word signs used in the titles of the programmes; in the UK to be 'a scouse' or from 'the valleys' carries a multitude of associations with respect to class. As we've noted before, these representations are not neutral, and 'class' itself is constructed in these narratives and presentations, as they are 'watched, discussed and *used* by people to make sense of the world and their place within it' (Allen and Mendick 2012: 472). These representations are thus not inconsequential, making class function in the social world beyond the programmes themselves.

With regard to gender, Angela McRobbie has noted that certain kinds of reality TV do 'symbolic violence' to women; not least in the advice given by middle-class lifestyle experts in programmes such as *What Not To Wear* (McRobbie 2004). McRobbie notes this symbolic violence as 'the public denigration by women of recognized taste (the experts and presenters) of women of little or no taste' (2004: 99). It is worth thinking about the larger discourses about gender that are being played out within reality TV output, and how they help construct attitudes in wider society. What do programmes such as *Four Weddings* (2009) and *One Born Every Minute* (2010) collectively tell us about what 'success' and 'aspiration' should look like for women? Such programmes perpetuate dominant ideological discourses about womanhood and motherhood. To extend the analysis of Rebecca L. Stephens (2004), they glorify highly conventional aspirations (motherhood, marriage) and might even be read as tapping into a rising sense of panic in society about what happens to those institutions as women become more independent. Dominant ideological discourses can be found in other reality TV shows also; *The Apprentice* can be seen to affirm particular conceptualizations of work, organization and competition as 'the norm', a norm where neoliberal ideals become common sense (Couldry and Littler 2008); the programme makers of *Benefits Street* (2014) in the UK were roundly chastised for playing into a dominant ideological discourse about those on welfare, when the programme had proposed to do quite the opposite; and *The Undateables* (2012) plays into everyday readings of difference even as it attempts to undermine and reconfigure them. Reality TV not only has a frustrated reality with the real then, but a frustrated relationship with democracy and public service also.

John Corner's critique of reality TV from 2002 still gives us pause for thought; what is reality TV's civic purpose he asks (John Corner 2002)? Reality TV that is designed solely to be entertaining is rarely radical, educational, inquisitive or useful in any sustained way. This is increasingly a worry given that we have a public service tradition that is on the decline, and a consumer society that is on the rise. This claim can be countered by noting that reality TV has been quite good in awareness-raising for some groups, most notably perhaps gay and transgender participant-contestants, or those with disabilities. Other programmes can be seen as having an interventionist role; eating better (*Supersize vs. Superskinny* 2008), staying healthy (*Embarrassing Bodies* 2007), or being pro-active within communities (*Secret Millionaire* 2006) (Ouellette 2010).

The scorecard – in representational terms – is very mixed indeed, and as such it is no wonder that reality TV has created such 'an extensive discursive field' (Deery 2015). But we might note that that discursive field perhaps misses the mark where it focuses on discussion of the genre's perceived superficiality and undermines and even misinterprets the role of the audience in constructing the text. As Annette Hill reminds us, 'Perhaps the people most in tune with reality TV today are the audiences... audiences are the experts' (2015: 15). We have seen that interpreting reality TV formats and the representations they offer up is fraught with difficulty, not least because we often arrive at the discussion with such weighted pre-conceptions and ideological positions with respect to reality TV's output.

The next chapter looks at a range of texts that couldn't be further from reality TV in terms of the attitudinal stances and assessments of cultural value that they usually provoke; not least the representations offered up as 'knowledge' in museums and at historic sites. Interestingly however, we will see many of the same discourses and problematics activated in the discussion.

NOTES

1 With a three-year concurrent sentence for reckless endangerment.
2 All dates correspond to first airing unless otherwise identified.

5

THE MEDIATED PAST

This chapter extends the range of cultural representations under analysis to include those found in museums and at historic sites, and to think about the representational qualities and responsibilities of their practice. This is the focus of the second half of this chapter. The first part focuses on the mediated past within other environments, considering how it appears and is made sense of in (for example) print, television, film, photography, radio and on the web.

German cultural critic and philosopher Walter Benjamin noted in 1940 that 'the past can be seized only as an image which flashes up at the instant when it can be recognized and is never seen again' (1940). Benjamin, whose writings are associated with the Frankfurt School of thought, wrote this piece in *On The Concept of History* at the start of 1940, before later that year killing himself to avoid capture by the Nazis. His writings are therefore poignant in any analysis of what the significance of the past, and our understanding of its role in the present, might be. In this quote he notes that the past is not something concrete and stable, which can be accessed through history books and remains unchanged and unchallenged over time. Rather, Benjamin saw it as something conjured up only in certain moments, that we *create* in the present, and that is then no longer accessible in the same way in other moments, or by other people. We *use* the past in different ways at different times, as will be seen in this chapter.

THE MEDIATED PAST

> It is safe to say, as we stand firmly established in the twenty-first century, that our engagement with history has become almost entirely mediated.
>
> (Garde-Hansen 2011: 1)

As Joanne Garde-Hansen points out in the quotation above, unlike with other aspects of culture that might be apparent to us in our day-to-day lives, our encounters with the past tend to be almost fully mediated in some way; through television programmes, films, search engines and the online encyclopedias which have become a first port of call for many in their historical inquiry. We have access to the past through a multitude of means that simply would not have been available even 50 years ago and should be suspicious of any assertion that history is the sum total of the contents of dedicated history books. Histories, as widely understood, have, according to Walkowitz and Knauer, been 'destabilized' and even 'discredited' (2009: 4) by this realization. In light of this, 'the past' becomes especially interesting in representational terms, although we might note that this area has seen less exploration in media and communications research than any other in this book. Within media *production* contexts however, it has been a very different story. In recent years (especially since the 1990s in Western contexts) we have seen an unprecedented interest in history across the media so that, according to Cannadine 'more history [is] being produced and consumed than ever before' (Cannadine 2004). There are a number of reasons that we might identify for that growth including a number of high profile events and commemorations, the millennium, or the Centenary of the start of World War I for example, but also events such as the death of Nelson Mandela, which encourage a certain amount of introspection and a concomitant turn to the past. There has also been a growth in interest in genealogy and family ancestry as records are released online, and increased access to technologies enabling their distribution and search. Websites such as Friends Reunited, Genes Reunited and even Facebook, have all encouraged further connection with our individual and shared pasts. The increase of historical content on television especially has reflected and encouraged increased connection with the past, and become the principal mechanism via which people encounter it. Few history books can reach the number of people a high profile historical drama can. Dawn Airey, a past Chief Executive of Channel 5 in the UK has said that history is 'the new sex' on television (Cannadine 2004).

The relationship between history and the media is a complex one; it might be said that media, history and memory are intertwined (Garde-Hansen 2011). That, as has already been noted, history is a key component of media output, but that media are increasingly a part of our histories, how we define, archive, and access them; how we 'know' they happened. Think for example of the first steps on the moon, or the events in New York on 11 September 2001. Our understanding of these events is completely inseparable from their mediatization. Indeed, as Cannadine notes, 'the history of the last hundred and more years, and also the history of our own time, is incomplete – indeed incomprehensible – without [the media]' (Cannadine 2004). As such, representations of history actually help to *create* history.

It is common to think of the media – especially print and television news, and perhaps now Twitter – as 'the first draft of history' (Garde-Hansen 2011). Understanding history as drafted, preliminary, and subject to revision, helps us conceive of it as a thing created. It does not 'exist' independently and objectively but is constructed through books, archival materials and the other resources we have at our disposal (those that survive over time at least). As such then, it is pertinent that we 'question the versions of the past presented' (Gray and Bell 2013: 2), and the perspectives and points of view they privilege. Lest we forget, we should query absences of history also. For example, questioning why news reporting and interpretation is so often presented in an absence of historical context and what the consequences of that might be (Cannadine 2004). When we see, hear or read stories in the media about the Israeli–Palestinian context, the absence of history can make it incredibly difficult for audiences to get a handle on what the parameters and implications of the particular news item are. We might deem that to be troubling if we are interested in informed and active citizens and political engagement.

Emergent in any analysis of representations of the past are a number of other tensions. First, a tension between what can and cannot be 'known' in relation to that past. Our understanding of the past is of course limited by our capacity to interpret from the evidence available to us. Such evidence gives us only a partial perspective. In some mediated pasts, such as documentaries, that partiality can be explored, but in others the gaps will need to be filled by media makers; they introduce fictional elements. More broadly, there are those historical narratives that are produced as non-fiction and presented as past tense, and others which are told in the present tense and almost fully fictionalized, such as drama. It is worth noting here that neither documentary nor drama is more 'true' or 'authentic' than the other, the distinction between fact and fiction being a touch misleading when it comes to interpretations of the past. There is another tension between the histories produced within academic environments by historians, and those produced within the media for what might be very different purposes and audiences. We might critique the media's capacity to open up history whilst simultaneously closing it down; mediations of the past propose that we take an interest in particular periods in history, at the same time as they tell us what to think about them, presenting only one narrative line (usually) through which we might encounter that past. They close it down in other ways also; limiting our perspectives to, say, those of the victors as opposed to the victims (in narratives about war for example), or of elites over and above the histories as experienced by ordinary people. There has been an attempt to redress this in light of Richard Hoggart's assessment of the 'everyday' as interesting in and of itself (1957), but our televisual pasts are still peppered with the stories of monarchs, well-to-do families and their 'help'. It is through these individuals that we are encouraged to encounter the past, rather than through the stories of groups and collectives who might provide a more full and complex picture. We might ask whether it is a fair assessment that the media *exploit* the past, using it as a means of arousing emotion in viewers in a manner that is manipulative at best. Has Hollywood appropriated the experiences of, say, the Rwandan people, the Scots, or those who were trafficked from Africa and sold as slaves in (respectively) *Hotel Rwanda* (2004), *Braveheart* (1995) and *10 Years A Slave* (2013)?

The fictionalizing charge is a serious one, as is the accusation that 'the past' often presented as a result is nostalgic and unhelpful. Holdsworth noted in 2011 that television especially 'has become a deeply nostalgic technology' (2011), presenting versions of the past that are unrecognizable, patronizing and offensive in their simplicity. Such representations, perhaps most ably demonstrated in internationally successful series like *Downton Abbey* (UK 2010), are characterized by longing for a time that was in some way better, or at least less difficult than the present. This is problematic, not least in light of developments with regard to human rights, working and living conditions, and equality. Such cosy and old-fashioned representations of the past might be understood as clichéd and, according to Jerome de Groot, 'uninterrogative' (2011). Boym notes that the charge of nostalgia in relation to programming has become 'an affectionate insult at best' (Boym 2001: xiv). Nostalgic renditions of the past might be deemed troubling in light of what they reveal about our attitudes within the present. Are we really of the opinion that the past presented in series such as *Call the Midwife* (UK 2012) is to be longed for? The 1950s was of course not a 'simpler' time; all periods must be assessed in light of the wider socio-political-cultural context. This period was one characterized by higher death rates, intense poverty, no access to the pill, limited (illegal) access to abortions, and paltry pain relief for expectant mothers. The soft focus rendition of 1950s London that is found in *Call the Midwife* has become hugely popular both in the UK and overseas, the yearning voiceover, the fashion, the music, the endless tea and cake consumed, and tender visions of community (everyone hanging their washing in rows) present a rather romanticized view of that period.

David Herman notes that the book the series is based on has itself been sanitized and made 'decent', losing references to race for

Figure 5.1 Call the Midwife, BBC

example that would have made modern audiences uncomfortable. He notes that 'We want a past that is cosy and better than today, the past we would like to remember, not the past as it actually was – golliwogs, domestic violence and all' (Herman 2013). Nostalgia programming has become big business, not least in advertising where the past has become a way of packaging and selling commodities. This is no better exemplified than in two high-profile UK campaigns: use of the image of Audrey Hepburn to sell Galaxy chocolate bars in 2013, and the not uncontroversial appropriation of the World War I Centenary to advertise Sainsbury's supermarket for their Christmas campaign 2014.

One area where we repeatedly see the past as in deficit is in relation to technology. On this theme the past is presented as dark, repressive, inferior and uncivilized. Those trying to solve crimes (for example) are not only disadvantaged but impaired by the reversal of 'progress'. It has been said that 'the past is a foreign country', and we might understand its inhabitants as 'Other'; it is through the prism of technology that the past's *difference* is perhaps most ably demonstrated.

In the examples we have looked at thus far, it is producers, scriptwriters, directors and researchers who have a responsibility for mediating the past, but we might note the rise in high-profile historians within this landscape also; David Starkey, Simon Scharma and Mary Beard for example. They have become some of the highest paid presenters on television, and their influence extends far beyond the programmes they front. They increasingly have an input in televised political discourses also, with all three being regular contributors on BBC *Question Time* and BBC Radio 4. The expansion of consumer culture and the cult of the celebrity has extended into history programming also.

We might ask how and why televisual representations of the past in particular connect so vividly with viewers. First there is the immediacy of the visual image, and the fact that within such a medium there is the *potential* for multiple viewpoints, on a contested issue for example. Then there is the added element of technical interpretation that is enabled within the formats it offers; computer reconstructions of the past, for example, are common. There is the potential for eye-witness testimony to be incorporated, or filmed footage from the past also. Such content connects emotionally with viewers and conveys a message very readily. As Ian Kershaw notes, television can communicate an inbuilt drama which is usually unmatched in a book or a lecture (Kershaw 2004). But televised representations of the past are often open to accusations of superficiality; they are fast-moving, often skim over the detail or problems of interpretation, and make detailed analysis problematic. This is one reason the charge of 'dumbing down' is often levied against such platforms. Within such contexts only certain kinds of history will be the foci, with some stories lending themselves better to the medium; dramatic, spectacular, macabre. For this reason it is no surprise that there is so much war on our screens. Television treatments are hostages to the archival materials at their disposal; so, an emphasis on twentieth-century narratives is more common than, say, representations of ancient Egypt, not least because we have compelling audio-visual documentation to work with.

Of course the majority of us now *consume* the past within a mixed and multiply layered mediascape, which raises questions about how we prioritize our sources of historical information (Kidd 2014). If we think for a moment about one historical narrative – the War on Terror – and how it has been mediated, we can reflect on how we might make sense of the different outputs, and how they come together to 'mashup' the past. The phrase 'War on Terror' was used by George W. Bush after the attack on the Twin Towers in 2001, and utilized by the press as a shorthand for a complex series of events and campaigns, until it was largely abandoned by politicians (by 2010). There are of course multiple news articles that make reference to the War on Terror, and these might be a reasonable start point for any investigation. Wikipedia also, and increasingly, has become a first port of call for information retrieval. The BBC has a micro-site dedicated to the War on Terror (now called Investigating al-Qaeda[1]), and the World Service made two documentaries called *The Secret War on Terror* in 2011. YouTube features a range of citizen responses to and overviews of the War on Terror such as Keaton Simons' news montage *Masters of War* set to a soundtrack of Bob Dylan. Adam Hodges' book *The 'War on Terror' Narrative* is a scholarly overview, whilst *War on Terror* is a first-person combat game for PC (2006). We might ask, which of the above interpretations of the 'War on Terror' is the most useful or appropriate? Does our assessment of that change over time, and in differing contexts? Our understanding of that past is contingent and relational, shifting depending on the media extensions that we draw on (Jenkins 2011).

As has been noted, representations of war are startlingly common. This is perhaps no great surprise, the narratives associated with war are epic, emotive and resonant. People's propensity to warmonger continues to fascinate, but presenting the nuance and 'reality' of war is of course an intense challenge. All too often, war can become a simple battle of good versus evil, where, according to Oscar-winning Producer Lord Puttnam, 'actions become completely divorced from consequences' (in Womack 2005). Jean Baudrillard's collection of essays *The Gulf War Did Not Take Place* is a provocation on these themes (1995). Baudrillard was of course not of the belief that the events of the First Gulf War hadn't taken place, rather, he sought to comment on the experience of the war for ordinary citizens; that for them the war was heavily mediated. Could those representations be seen as the 'truth' of the war? Were they comparable to the event of war itself? Was the whole thing mere propaganda? Where were the Iraqi dead in the reporting? Baudrillard concluded that as we only saw the events of the Gulf War via the media, it did not happen; it was not a real but a virtual war, hyperreal and simulated. It has become common to talk about representations of war in such terms, not least with respect to the narrative worlds constructed in video games. Indeed, Alec Charles notes that 'It is not just that the virtual and the non-virtual are becoming indistinguishable; what is significant is that the non-virtual is increasingly subordinated to the virtual' (2012: 73). As such, 'the distinctions between the video game of the war and the war of the video game have significantly blurred' (Charles 2012: 78). Such analyses also expose how video games are now used within a variety of contexts to educate people about war, not least in educational environments and the military. *America's Army* (Figure 5.2) is a platform produced as 'The official U.S. Army game' to deliver:

> stunningly realistic environments, lighting effects, animations, and team-based experiences so that America's Army players can experience the training, teamwork and values that give American Soldiers Strength Like No Other.
>
> (U.S. Army, undated)

We can begin to critique the discourse at play here; are the environments 'realistic'? What is meant by 'experience'? What are

Figure 5.2 America's Army 3, 2009, U.S. Army

American 'values'? What or who constitutes the 'team'? Why strength 'like no other'? In representational terms the lexical choices here are of course loaded and potentially problematic. Since 2002 a number of iterations of the gameplay have been played by more than 10 million people; new recruits to the 'elite America's Army team'. This kind of gamified introduction to the Army is seen as a compelling, immersive and familiar introduction to close quarters combat in an environment that can speak to a generation raised on games. We can imagine the end-goals of the makers; awareness-raising yes, but also recruitment, public relations, and uncritical support.

Many mediations of war might be open to accusations of sanitization and/or simplification, but one film over others has been heralded as providing a sea change in representations. Anyone who has watched the *Saving Private Ryan* scenes depicting the D-Day landing on Omaha beach will recall their intensity and vividness, even graphicness. Director Steven Spielberg sought to create a representation that veterans would recognize and so broke many conventions. Camera shots hold the viewer's gaze on disaster for longer than is comfortable, a bewildering number of casualties are depicted, with most being American which was unprecedented in representational terms. The lense is blurred with water and blood, the audio fades in and out, the sound of the bullets is piercing. The scene is an absolute assault on the senses, and signalled a new treatment of historical subject matter. Paris notes that 'Spielberg's aim was to bring the audience as close as possible to the experience of being in combat, even if he risked alienating some viewers in the process' (Paris 2007).

Yet as we know, true accuracy of representation is an illusion when you are dealing with the past, and Spielberg's treatment is ultimately a treatment like any other. Mediations of the past are dependent on incomplete narratives and judgements of value that have been made over and again since that time we seek to represent. They are not neutral, and can in fact be intensely political. None more so than those representations on offer in museums and heritage contexts, the subject of the remainder of this chapter.

THE MUSEOLOGICAL PAST

A museum is most readily understood as architecturally and materially grounded in the institution. Museums' physicality – often grandiose and even intimidating – is apparent before visitors even step through the door, and it remains core to their function that they collect, archive and display *things*; things that are given meaning and status simply through their institutionalization. But museums are about more than just buildings and artefacts, they have at their nexus texts, images and ideas also. We might note that (increasingly) museums tell their stories through computer screens and interactives, have virtual presences, and can be seen as in the business of communication, storytelling, even broadcasting (Kidd 2014). Although the domain of museums is not solely representations of the past, such representations are clearly a significant part of their remit; museums are demonstrable sites in which we encounter 'the past'. Although not always on the radar of media and communications scholars, museums' significance should not go unnoticed. According to Saur there were 55,000 museums in 202 countries in 2011, a figure that will have been superseded as their number grows all of the time, not least in China where there are thousands of new museums (*The Economist* 2013). Museums are key constituents in the making of meaning as regards to identity, community and nation. Their history, and their role within nation-building, and nation-branding, is well documented (Bennett 1995). In 2015 there are museums dedicated to just about everything: The Pencil Museum (Keswick, England), the SPAM® Museum (Austin, Minnesota), the Underwater Museum (Cancun, Mexico), the Condom Museum (Nonthaburi, Thailand) and the Museum of Broken Relationships dedicated to failed relationships and their 'ruins' (Zagreb, Croatia). Yet we will see in this chapter that museums are intensely challenging with regard to the politics of representation (Kidd et al. 2014, Cameron and Kelly 2010); they are live sites of struggle, with their own discursive formations (Foucault 1980).

With reference to the first half of this chapter, we might note that a museum or gallery visit does not stand alone as an act of cultural consumption. Invariably our expectations of the visit and our experiences therein will be framed by other mediations of the heritage on offer (Glassberg 1986). For example, if I visit Hampton Court Palace (England, Historic Royal Palaces) to find out more about the life of Henry VIII and his wives, that visit will invariably be informed by other representations of those individuals from other media; fictional and non-fictional books, films and television programmes, and of course by information I might find on the Internet. People do not arrive at heritage sites as 'blank slates' upon which the past will be written (Burton and Scott 2003).

I have noted ways in which museums might be comparable to other forms of media; they script, edit, select, design and commission blockbusters, they use a multitude of audio-visual features, and just like documentary makers or journalists, they tell stories. Michelle Henning characterizes the museum as a 'hybrid space' full of technology (2005: 152) and Angelina Russo has asserted that 'the contemporary museum is a media space' (2012: 145). We might note that museums include and they exclude, they make certain ways of viewing the world more likely than others; as such, they are far from neutral or safe spaces.

But the museum is also a different site of representation for a number of reasons. First, as has been noted, their physicality is striking. Museums display physical embodiments of the past as 'evidence' that fosters remembering and engagement. Museums turn 'things' into 'objects' (Henning 2005: 7, but also Dicks 2003, Kirshenblatt-Gimblett 1998), a process that is infused with power as layers of interpretation and significance are attached to what then becomes an 'artefact'. Second, within museum and heritage contexts, we tend not to talk about 'audiences' or 'users' (although these terms might be increasingly applicable, especially online), but about 'visitors' instead. The difference is more than mere semantics. 'Visiting' or *being* a visitor again asserts the physicality of the experience, the movement from A to B, and then back to A again. Being a visitor means temporarily inhabiting someone else's space or story; moving *through* it as opposed to moving *in*. It is an active status, and it is also one characterized by multiplicity, visitors are simultaneously other things as well; tourists, school pupils, students, researchers. People perform multiple identities in the place and space of the museum. Third, museums almost universally have learning at the heart of their mission. Museums have very clear education remits for reaching both formal and informal learners. They often have dedicated education staff, programmes, physical spaces and online portals. Like broadcasters with a public service remit, education does go hand-in-hand with entertainment, but the former is often seen as the more worthwhile and noble activity within museum spaces. The embodied and experiential quality of a museum visit is difficult to ascertain, but there is no doubting that the discourse of 'experience' and immersion has become vital in the pursuit of visitors. This extends to the other facilities provided within museum spaces; cafes, restrooms and shops for example. Their presence is not incidental.

So what is it that museums do aside from these commitments to education and experience? We have already noted the responsibility museums have to collect, archive and preserve artefactual heritage. This is a responsibility that now extends into the digital domain; online collections are ubiquitous for museums and galleries, with many recognizable gameplayers being forerunners within that space; Google's Art Project for example, which includes high-resolution digital images of artworks from the Rijksmuseum in Amsterdam, the Museum of Modern Art in New York, the State Hermitage Museum in Russia and Tate Britain in London (amongst others). Whether museums are actively collecting or not, their duty of care for the artefacts in their possession is of course central to their cultural and curatorial role. It is here that things become more interesting for us in representational terms, not least as they link to patterns and practices of display. In constructing a museum display judgements have to be made about whose heritages will be presented and in what way. As Henrietta Lidchi notes, the display of objects is a system of representation which works to produce meaning (1997). When 'choosing' artefacts for display in order to speak to particular histories, complex decisions (or value judgements) must be made about the overall look and feel of the collection, its display context, and even whether to charge for the privilege of engaging with it. Decisions also have to be made about which interpretation of an object is the correct or preferred one to present to visitors. In this respect, the polysemic nature of artefacts as texts is ignored; that is, their ability to have many meanings. Objects are displayed out of their original contexts, and will regularly undergo some form of reconstruction themselves (conservation for example) that renders large periods of the item's past undesirable. It is often only within its original form that an object is seen as maintaining its truth. Conservation sees it as possible, even desirable, to undo the past. We might like to think about the kinds of objects that are preserved over time; fragments of porcelain, but also weaponry and coins. There are of course very many materials that do *not* survive the test of time, so we can see that our understanding of the past as interpreted from the fragments that endure will of course be skewed and partial.

Bringing objects together within a display context is asking them to work together to tell some kind of story. Putting them next to one another in a museum tells visitors that there is a connection between them of some kind and there is of course a politics in this. If I put the Ukrainian flag in a museum display next to some images of Ukrainian food, they combine to tell one story. If I put that flag next to the Russian flag, it tells a very different story. The whole cultural and political narrative shifts quite considerably. When you stop and take note, you see some very strange juxtapositions of things in museums. There are also notable interpretive absences. Figure 5.3 of the sculpture in bronze, *Bust of Said Abdullah of the Darfour People* from 1848 is striking not only as an example of incredibly skilled craftsmanship, but due to the rarity of the subject as captured within this particular form, and then displayed within a gallery context (it is now on display in the Chicago Art Institute).

The acquisition of items by museums – their accessioning – is of course itself also political and linked to issues of representation. What to acquire, and how much to pay for it, continue to be divisive questions. We now consider past practices of collection to be ethically very dubious and troubling. Collectors on imperial missions in the Empire brought back objects of note from all over the world; they took, stole, or were gifted them for private collections. These were later absorbed into public collections, and eventually put on display so that a limited section of the population could encounter them. There continues to be much debate about whether such objects should be returned to their point of

Figure 5.3 Charles-Henri-Joseph Cordier, *Bust of Said Abdullah of the Darfour People*, 1848, Bronze, H. 82.5 cm (32 1/2 in.) (with socle), Ada Turnbull Hertle Endowment, 1963.839, The Art Institute of Chicago. Photography © The Art Institute of Chicago

origin, and under what conditions. The re-introduction of cultural works to their originating context – their repatriation – remains very rare. There is a concurrent discussion also about how to acknowledge the complex legacies of objects' colonial origins, as Geraldine Kendall notes in an article for the U.K. Museums Association's journal:

> how can institutions founded to display the spoils of empire stay relevant in a postcolonial world – and how far should they go to acknowledge their sometimes disreputable histories?
>
> (Kendall 2013)

There is (perhaps understandably) a huge amount of resistance from museums on this subject, with the exception perhaps of objects classified as human remains where there has been some movement to return objects (especially to Aboriginal and Māori communities). The enduring fear is that beginning to return objects will open a floodgate of requests from source communities that would see the Museums of Europe and Northern America emptied. It would spell the end of what have rather curiously been termed 'encyclopaedic' museums. In the legal debates that circulate around these cultural artefacts, they are re-configured as 'cultural property' that can be owned. In a provocative article for *Foreign Affairs* in 2014 James Cuno called for an end to 'frivolous restitution claims' and the 'claim game', but the high profile debate over the ownership of the Parthenon Marbles (for example) shows that this issue is unlikely to go away. There is much debate about whether the British Museum's 'ownership' of these Greek sculptures – from the Acropolis in Athens – is legal, and a fierce campaign continues to see them returned.[2] The British Museum holds steadfast in its position that the stones belong at a site which houses all of the world's great culture, and that their return would set an alarming precedent. Curiously perhaps, given the high profile nature of the debate about the Marbles, there is no mention of their contested ownership in their online database entry although there is a leaflet you can pick up in the physical gallery itself. It seems unlikely that the integrity of the collection in Athens will be restored in the near future at least.

Museums display a host of difficult objects, perhaps none more so than the slave shackles that pervade museum collections. A slave shackle is of course not just an object. It is infused with power, politics, hate, anger, sadness, and a great weight. It might mean different things to different people. How is the complexity of an object such as this to be portrayed in the limited space and linguistic resources available for a small text panel? It is not uncommon to find a complete failure to engage with the complexity. I have seen a slave chain presented in amongst a pile of other products of the iron age as just another bit of iron, with no mention of its connection to slavery. Is that responsible display? Slave shackles might in the past have been used to tell a more triumphal story of course; their meaning is not stable over time. This raises the larger question about what the ramifications of exhibiting the Other might be within museums, and these are revisited in the following section.

The use of human remains within museum displays is a live issue also; how are the dead displayed as 'Other'? Skeletons and preserved bodies (mummies, bog bodies and the like) are all frequent fixtures within the museum experience, and we don't often stop to think about the ethical ramifications of their display. This is perhaps because those remains are mostly from pasts which we might deem ancient. When it comes to more recent pasts, our attitudes might be different. What about the display of human remains from World War II, or the Rwandan Genocide? In 2015 the burial of the remains of Richard III in Leicester, England, was the subject of intense media interest and scrutiny, with much being made of the contestation about how and where his remains should be reinterred after being found in a car park in the city in 2012. How we deal with human remains, and the fascination they hold for members of the public and the media, is a subject worthy of increased scholarly reflection.

Another of the roles performed within museums is that of classification. Such an activity would seem pretty benign and even mundane, but is of course itself also political. The classification of animals into species according to their characteristics is not controversial, and can be a useful way of organizing and identifying them. But when that is extended to the classification of humans, we become rather more squeamish. The most infamous example of this is the principle of eugenics which was emergent within a number of contexts during the twentieth century. Eugenics is a philosophy that seeks to encourage the high reproduction of people with sets of characteristics that are deemed positive, and the converse, lower breeding amongst those with less desirable characteristics. Nazi Germany is the most notable example of the philosophy made state policy. The Nazis pursued an idea of an Aryan race with particular physical characteristics, and used eugenics as a basis for their racial policies. They employed inhumane methods of measurement in order to try and eliminate other races and those with mental and physical disabilities. This was only possible because the Nazis subscribed to the idea that certain races (for example) have particular genetic factors that are inevitably and always present, and could be classified. In this context, classification became intensely political, and its consequences profound. Classification is not a neutral process.

Within museum encounters then, there are a number of questions that we should ask with regard to representation: How are the various media available on site being used to construct a version of the past? Does it matter whether what we see in museums is 'real' or 'authentic'? What are the 'limits or representation' within museums? Whose interpretations are being privileged? What can be known about past peoples from their weaponry, food, belief systems, skulls, physiology? Is knowledge the sum of these parts? Is a gallery just a random collection of stuff placed in juxtaposition or does it amount to more than that? If so, what?

REPRESENTING THE OTHER IN MUSEUMS

So who is this 'Other' and how are museums implicated in their representation? In different ways and in different contexts of course, that Other could be any one of us. We make sense of our selves, and our identities through principally unconscious processes of 'Othering'. Othering refers to the practices of distinction and difference that give us access to identity. So, to be white only makes sense in its distinction from being black, being male only works as it notes the difference from female, to be disabled is to be 'other' than able-bodied. Processes of Othering teach us about who we are, what we stand for, and what we might reasonably expect from life. The concept helps us define ourselves. As Stuart Hall says 'Difference signifies. It "speaks".'

Othering works through binary oppositions: good versus bad, desirable versus undesirable, civilized versus primitive:

> in defining their own sense of identity, individuals and groups tend to fix the identity of others, often working within long-established binary codes of thinking that help sustain inequalities, exclusions and oppression.
>
> (Weedon 2004: 154)

Othering is then about how we define ourselves, but by extension, it also impacts on how we define and understand people more broadly. 'Difference' is a positive and a negative thing – we **need** it to identify ourselves from others. It is **necessary** for the production of meaning. It's how we know ourselves, define and articulate what we are about. I'm not a pensioner. I'm not a goth. But at the same time, it is threatening – it has negative implications. It can lead to hostility and aggression towards the Other. Them.

Cultural theorist Stuart Hall was particularly concerned with Othering as related to race, and we might note how problematic a notion 'race' is. As much as race is often taken to be indicated at a biological level, that is not in fact true. There is nothing inherent about race; race, as with other semiotic meanings, is applied. It is as a result of politics, history and power that we attach so much significance to skin colour, and often see 'whiteness' as a naturalized and universal 'normal' from which everyone else is seen to deviate, even at the same time as white people are in fact a global minority. As such, whiteness is an incredibly powerful cultural construct (not, as we have noted, biologically determined). It is against this norm that all others are invited to define themselves. We might note that white people are seldom articulated as 'white', they are just 'are'. In news stories, if somebody is white they are invariably not identified as such in text. Model. Writer. Director. As opposed to Black model. Black writer. Black director. White people eat food. Theirs is not 'ethnic food'. They wear clothes. Theirs is not 'ethnic fashion' (Storey 2009). John Storey says that 'By not being "raced", they become the human race' (Storey 2009).

As we noted, Figure 5.3 is remarkable for a number of reasons. One reason it might jar with our expectations for images of African subjects is in its treatment of the black body. Here the black body – the torso and head – are clothed. The pose is majesterial. Each individual hair is hand crafted in great detail. The subject's features are dignified and strong. To be in the gallery space with the bust at the Chicago Institute of Art is to be alive to its presence. This is not a typical representation of the black body. When we think about the black body as it is represented in the media and culture, we might note a few common images: The black body as athlete is a common image; the black body as exotic (as in, say, the many images in *National Geographic* magazine); the black body as nude, or starving (see images in the news, or circulated as part of the Live Aid campaign); the black body as incarcerated (as in the many documentaries about African-Americans in prisons); the black body as sexualized (images circulated in pornographic output). Mercer said in 1999 that 'the essence of the black male lies in the domain of sexuality and there is a long pedigree of writing – including from Stuart Hall – that is in agreement. Hall famously asserted that black sexuality was itself seen as Other, excessive, threatening, fixing the black man at the level of the genitals. He pointed to a white fascination with black sexuality, quoting psychiatrist and philosopher Frantz Fanon as saying: 'One is no longer aware of the Negro, but only of a penis; the Negro is eclipsed' (in Hall 1997: 290). Black women's bodies similarly have been fetishized and objectified; she is dismantled, confined to the level of body parts, open for voyeuristic activity.

So why do we find ourselves in a situation of such problematic representation of black people? To explore this question we need to look at the origins of racialized representation (see Storey 2009). The basic vocabularies that people use for talking about race were produced under systems of slavery and the slave trade, and have changed very little since that time. In order to defend those systems, which we now see as barbaric and inhumane, it was necessary to establish an understanding of black people, especially Africans, as different, as Other. If those enslaved were seen as 'the same' as their owners and traders, their continued subjugation could *not* have been argued for. They had to be 'inferior', and the way of articulating that was through absolute difference between white and black. This ideology became more widespread of course because it was not only those directly involved with slavery and the slave trade that benefitted from it – the wider public had discovered a taste for sugar from the sugar plantations, a commodity they had not been able to readily access previously. So here we see most bleakly the work of 'Othering', its uses and its consequences.

In the eighteenth century slavery on plantations was widespread, and only beginning to be questioned. The continuation of slavery even in the face of a growing abolitionist movement into the nineteenth century was only possible because of the racialized discourse that surrounded it. That whites were civilized, cultured, pure, refined, learned, and blacks were instinctual, unpredictable, emotional, lacking in intellect and unable to control their sexual urges, leading to 'pollution' of the white race. The very visibility of this difference in the black body, the fact that you could see it, became an evidence of sorts that those things were 'true'. This ideology led many White Europeans to regard themselves as the only people able to think and govern in any meaningful way, and they went on to set up colonies around the globe through practices of conquest and colonialization. The white European was on a mission to 'civilize' the world, to 'humanize' the Other (Storey 2009).

Images of racial difference emerged during the nineteenth century as a result of the imperial encounter. The image of Africa in particular, was as a mysterious place, one not civilized but something Other; primitive. And so we see that binary in operation. This was concretized in the selection of material artefacts that were brought back by private collectors to Western contexts, and that eventually made their way into museum collections. Ethnography and cultural anthropology – attempts to observe and study societies other than one's own – were key constituencies in the birth of collections and of museums. Being able to exhibit 'the Other' made it of course easier to make an argument for 'nation' and 'identity' as fixed in the host's context (through *'différance'*, Derrida 1967), and these continue to be key ambitions of museums (Bennett 1995).[3] As a result of that colonial past, museums, in Europe especially, continue to hold vast ethnographic collections. According to a Wikipedia search (April 2015) the University of Cambridge's ethnography and anthropology collections contain 800,000 objects, the Pitt Rivers Museum in Oxford houses 500,000 such objects and the British Museum holds 350,000 objects. Collections that include such things as shrunken heads and other bodily remains are of course intensely problematic in representational terms. They run the risk of representing the Other in very limited terms; as exotic, spectacular, and marked by difference.

What we have seen in museums in recent years is an attempt to diversify their practice with regard to representation, programmes and governance. It is common for museums to have advisory panels populated by members of local and source communities, to respond to wider initiatives such as Black History Month or African-American History Month (every October in Canada, the United States and the UK), and to host debates and exhibitions which respond to the provocation that museums continue to be implicated in the exploitation and mis-representation of minorities that are the legacies of colonialism. Such attempts seek to move beyond the tokenistic, and are often sophisticated interpretive ventures. Discourses of participation, collaboration, co-production and social justice are now significant in the museological lexicon. Museums move slowly, but they are at least headed in the right direction.

One of the barriers to more movement to re-balance representations within museum contexts has been the paralyzing anxiety that museum professionals often feel in the face of the gravity of these issues (Kidd et al. 2014). Who are they to speak for the 'Other'? It is notable that black and minority ethnic groups remain significantly under-represented in the profession, and on postgraduate courses in museological disciplines. Nonetheless we should consider whether members of those communities would inevitably be able to speak authentically and unproblematically *on behalf* of that group. Is it reasonable to expect that a black woman would automatically be able to adequately speak on behalf of all black women? Such an assertion would ignore the polysemous character of communities; their discordances and frictions. But that observation does not divest museums of the responsibility for thinking ethically about how and on what grounds they 'Other'. Indeed, we should remind ourselves again that Othering is a characteristic of identity construction and relates to a broader spectrum of attachments than 'race'. Our understandings of race and racism infuse our everyday encounters in the world, not only our encounters of museums. This chapter is another of those encounters. Without stopping to notice that, we fail in our duty to create more *human* relationships:

> one question, one principle above all, emerges as a lesson for us. It is the fear – the terrifying internal fear – of living with *difference*. This fear arises as the consequence of the fatal coupling of difference and power. And, in that sense, the work that cultural studies has to do is mobilize everything that it can in terms of intellectual resources in order to understand what keeps making the lives we live, and the societies we live in, profoundly and deeply antihuman in their capacity to live with difference.
>
> (Hall 1997: 343)

NOTES

1 http://news.bbc.co.uk/1/hi/in_depth/world/2001/war_on_terror/default.stm, accessed January 2015.

2 This campaign (see www.marblesreunited.org.uk, www.parthenoninternational. org, www.bringthemback.org, accessed January 2015) has become more high profile in recent years due to the involvement of Amal Clooney, a lawyer and activist who, in 2014, married one of Hollywood's highest earning actors and producers, George Clooney.

3 In 2015, one of the key concerns as regards to cultural heritage is the destruction of sites and artefacts of historical significance by the group Islamic State in Iraq and Syria. The deliberate destruction of such sites is carefully orchestrated, and often filmed for propaganda purposes. IS are aware of the link between heritage, identity and nation, and the power of the image of such destruction to deliver their message. See Rose-Greenland and Müge Göçek (2014) for more on such 'cultural violence'.

6

SUBVERSIVE AND ALTERNATIVE
MEDIA MESSAGES

This chapter closes the book with a look at representations that
seek to subvert the dominant or hegemonic readings of texts
(Hall 1973) by opening them up to alternative meanings and
interpretations. These are examples of what can be seen as counter-
cultural representations, working in opposition to the mainstream
images and discourses that are offered up by our media and
creative industries; representations that are in some way oppositional to the cultural norm. It includes an overview of a range of
alternative media output, linking it to the wider embrace of user-
creativity and the maker movement. It will look at a range of
examples including subvertising, yarnbombing and the work of
the British artist Banksy. It will close with a look at the mainstream media response to these activities concluding that the
struggle for meaning remains an ongoing and intensely political
concern. The battle for control over the representations that are
allowed to circulate continues to be fought.

BACKDROP: JOHN FISKE'S JEANING OF AMERICA

In his book *Understanding Popular Culture* John Fiske opens with
a chapter on what he calls 'the jeaning of America', referencing
the ubiquity of jeans and questioning why that might have come to
be the case. There are of course logical reasons, he notes, for the
wearing of jeans; they fulfil a need for an informal, reasonably
neutral and hard-wearing wardrobe staple. But beyond that,
according to Fiske, we wear them to access a number of different
associations and representations of self that they are seen to
enable; to differentiate ourselves perhaps (there are many different
types of jeans) or to demonstrate our allegiance to a particular
brand (as in, say, Levi's), or to access some version of 'cool'. Many
of you will be wearing jeans as you read this; think for a moment
about your reasons why. Some of those will be associated with the
'material function' of jeans to keep us warm and comfortable, but
others will be associated more with 'meanings and values'; the
'cultural function' of jeans (Fiske 1990: 11). It is important not
only to look at a commodity's role in the circulation of wealth, or
in terms of its political economy, but to look also at its role in
the circulation of ideas, meanings and cultural norms. Such commodities are of course a part of the rich tapestry of source materials
from which we construct our identities, and our social relations.
Like the other texts that we have analyzed in this book, they
are not neutral. Jeans were a particularly interesting commodity
for Fiske to have targeted because of their ubiquity and
pervasiveness.

In his analysis Fiske goes on to assert that the wearing of jeans
is not characterized by freedom and differentiation in actual fact,
but rather that the very 'façade of ordinariness' they construct
actually *prohibits* self-expression. He asserts in his study that jeans
have the potential to be repressive, not least psychologically
(Fiske 1990: 2). If we look at the classic jean, Levi's 501 perhaps,
the self-promoted 'original jean', we might conclude that this is
true. That one's ability to self-express might be prohibited by the
very significance of the jeans themselves, their reputation giving
them meaning, as opposed to anything the wearer does. Perhaps a
reasonable conclusion might be that they *are* repressive. But Fiske

goes down another avenue which I think is of interest here as we come to a close in our study of representation. It transpires that he is less interested in the ways jeans *limit* our self-expression, than in the ways that they have been used as source materials for other kinds of activity and expression, and what the consequences of those forms of expression might be. Take the humble 501, created in the 1890s, and eventually the world's best selling clothing item. Over the years people have used their 501s as source materials through which to express their own meanings and resistances, treating them as blank canvases rather than finished and unpenetrable:

> If today's jeans are to express oppositional meanings, or even to gesture toward such social resistance, they need to be disfigured in some way – tie-dyed, irregularly bleached, or, particularly, torn. If 'whole' jeans connote shared meanings of contemporary America then disfiguring them becomes a way of distancing oneself from those values.
>
> (Fiske 1990: 4)

In using the very products of material capitalism and disrupting them through tearing and other creative practices, a commentary can be made about the values of the original.

However, Fiske observes how quick manufacturers are to cotton on to this kind of activity and to seek to commodify it. In the case of 501s, it wasn't long before Levi's were selling pre-faded, pre-torn and pre-dyed jeans themselves. Levi's 501 has even sold, and sparked a wider trend for, jeans pre-loaded with 'Anti-Fit' (as in Figure 6.1) so as to look good when worn in a bigger size; not to fit the body but to hang on it instead. In the embrace of the rebellious fashions of their users, the potential for more radical or oppositional meanings associated with (say) wearing jeans that are ripped or baggy is neutralized, and astutely turned into an opportunity for the sale of *more* goods; ripping then extends and enhances consumerism rather than providing a critique of it.

To Fiske, this could be seen as a process of the *incorporation* of oppositional texts and languages, adopting resistant practices and

Figure 6.1 Levi's campaign, 2005, UK, reproduced courtesy of The Advertising
Archives

in so-doing neutralizing their radical potential, or, it could be
seen as a process of *containment*; an attempt to restrict the activity,
dictate how a product is used, and demonstrate the mainstream's
ability to deal effectively with dissent and protest (Fiske 1990:
18). The latter is clearly a more hostile and cynical perspective.
Either way, the end result is that those who subscribe to alternative ideologies and worldviews have to find new ways of writing
them onto the goods available to them, which they do:

> Despite nearly two centuries of capitalism, subordinated subcultures
> exist and intransigently refuse finally to be incorporated – people in
> these subcultures keep devising new ways of tearing their jeans.
>
> (Fiske 1990: 19)

This actually is a rather creative tension, one that opens up culture as a site of play and experiment, as movable and shifting, cyclical and endlessly innovating. What becomes very apparent in Fiske's analysis is that popular culture is a mutable and inconsistent site of contradiction, its meanings not fixed, or singular. Here, the semiotic resources we are presented with, in this case jeans, are continually re-inscribed with contrary and even controversial meanings. And so Fiske gives us a model for thinking about how counter-cultural activities emerge and are institutionalized over time. This is a model that will be re-visited variously in the remainder of this chapter in a range of examples which explore attempts to subvert and disrupt mainstream representations. I begin with an introduction to alternative media, and an overview of the discourses that are activated in debate about them.

ALTERNATIVE MEDIA

Lately, communication scholarship has presented us with a different, more optimistic perspective: audiences are not totally powerless against the mass media ... Reception – says a soothing voice of solace – is a creative and active cultural process.

(Rodriguez 2001: 25)

The above citation recognizes – and celebrates – changing attitudes toward audiences that Clemencia Rodriguez and others were identifying toward the close of the twentieth century. The acknowledgement of 'active audiences' had become a staple of postmodern discourses, not least since Roland Barthes' essay *The Death of the Author* (1977) which posited that the traditional role of the author was becoming redundant. Traditional analyses of literature that concentrated on the author and their intended reading of a text were, to Barthes, a simplification of the process of authoring and narrating. In reality, according to Barthes, a disconnection occurs, 'the voice loses its origin' in the moment of utterance. Thus, the power of the text lies in the uses made by readers, it is opened up in the act of reading to any interpretation (Barthes 1977). Reading – audiencing – was being recognized as an agentic pursuit. John Downing (1988) concludes that audiences are capable of more than just rejecting media messages as identified in Stuart Hall's encoding/decoding model of communications (1980). In Downing's conceptualization, audiences not only have the capacity to work on and mould media in their practices of reception, but should be recognized as having a right of reply also; they can go as far as creating *alternative* media very much in opposition to that of the mainstream. His particular interest was in the 'alternative public sphere' that arose around and out of the anti-nuclear debate following the volatile political situation of the 1960 and 1970s. At this time an 'alternative' discourse was enabled by the increased availability of small-scale media technologies which resulted in wider public knowledge of political activism and its various outputs. Downing concentrates his argument on events in West Germany and Britain showing how in both contexts 'implicitly and often explicitly' there was a move to 'create models of media operation transcending the typical behaviour both of capitalist media conglomerates and of Soviet-style "transmission-belt" media' (Downing 1988: 163). Due to restrictions on traditional media and a shrinkage in the information exchanged and discussed in the public sphere (as predicted by Habermas 1994) political activists were forced to look to alternative media routes in order to deliver their messages. Current methods of public opinion formation were too restrictive, the power structure encroaching on the realm of public critical and rational debate. There had been a 'colonization of the life-world' resulting in a dilution of true public opinion (Downing 1988: 165). Downing further developed his theories about what he went on to call 'radical media' in a 2001 book, defining that term as 'media, generally small-scale and in many different forms, that express an alternative vision to hegemonic policies, priorities and perspectives' (Downing et al. 2001: v). Radical media were understood as media that attempted to 'break somebody's rules' (Downing et al. 2001: xi) being often organized more democratically than other organizations, and making attempts to voice excluded people's stories and opinions. Chris Atton's 2002 study of the changing face of these radical or alternative media forms built upon the work of Downing. His 'alternative media' is defined as that which offers 'the means for democratic communication to people who are normally excluded from media production' (Atton 2002: 4) in a process that blurs the polarized positions of 'alternative and mainstream ... powerful and powerless, dominance and resistance' (Atton 2002: 6). In Atton's view, words associated with the publishing industry which limited participation – such as 'print run' and 'distribution' – were soon to become obsolete (Atton 2002: 134). His assessments would prove prophetic.

Radical or alternative media often provide facts to the public that might otherwise be denied and 'explore fresh ways of developing a questioning perspective on the hegemonic process ... increasing the public's sense of confidence in its power to engineer constructive change' (Downing et al. 2001: 16). In the case of the media, this involves questioning the methods through which we consent to be 'given' media, and increasing the belief amongst 'audiences' that they could create more relevant and challenging content themselves. Alternative media have been termed many things in academic literature published since the millennium, 'radical', 'independent', 'citizens', 'activist', 'participatory', 'autonomous', 'grassroots', 'community' and, not unproblematically, 'democratic'. This is not to say that all such terms are interchangeable, there are 'significant nuances' in each of these lexical choices (Pickard 2007) but the range of terms does at least indicate the diversity of practice and the claims that are being made on its behalf (Atton 2002, Coyer et al. 2007, Bailey et al. 2008, Rodriguez et al. 2010). At the heart of all of these referents is a shared understanding that what is important is 'media resistance' (Dowmunt and Coyer 2007: 1).

Bailey, Cammaerts and Carpentier (2008) identify four different alternative media approaches that are interesting to note here with regard to representation. First, they identify alternative media practices that serve communities (not solely understood in geographical terms). These are forms of alternative media that have participation and access at their core, but that are often misconstrued solely as small-scale and local endeavours. The second set of approaches understand alternative media through direct comparison to mainstream media. Here, alternative media are seen as a 'supplement to' or as a 'counter-hegemonic critique of' the mainstream of media output. They produce and circulate 'non-conformist' representations (Bailey et al. 2008: 17), and are often also organizationally different from the mainstream, being less hierarchical and dominated by elites. In the third and fourth approaches, alternative media are linked to the concept of the civil society; a space occupied by non-governmental interests and separate from the market and thus one within which 'alternative conceptualisations of the political and economic system can develop and thrive' (Bailey et al. 2008: 21). Here we can see how alternative media might be interesting with regard to the study of representation; diversifying both the content and production of media, and opening up channels for expression to those who are under or mis-represented within mainstream media output. Atton notes that at their core alternative media are 'about offering the means for democratic communication to people who are normally excluded from media production' (Atton 2002: 4). Alternative media approaches tend to embrace subjectivity and individuals' storytelling, are often crowd-based, and try to inspire direct action. This has clear linkages into our theme of representation, indicating a possibility for people to become involved in the practices and processes of their own visibility; glimpsing at a more democratic and inclusive representational field. All of this brings us very abruptly back to issues of power, which have of course been a central tenet of this book.

To sum up (or perhaps crudely caricature) the differences between mainstream and alternative media, we might surmise the following: *Mainstream media* are largely commercial, often with business models centred on advertising, making their output vulnerable to corporate interests and distortion by capitalist agendas. Such media providers can be rather conservative with their output, tend not to be concerned with social values or public good (with the exception of public service media), are hierarchical, exclusive, and professionalized. As such, the majority of people remain structurally excluded and exhibit no power over the circulation of representations of themselves or of others. This is a consequence of the organizing logics of the media as business, but is also a mythical construct which alienates, as Dowmut and Coyer point out:

> the myth that 'the media' have managed to sell us (very effectively) is that they occupy a central space in society that is somehow magically

separated from us. So only a very few of us are 'in the media'; most of us are outside it and the 'place of media power' excludes us, seemingly naturally.

(Dowmunt and Coyer 2007: 4)

Alternative media, in contrast, are understood as having rather different agendas and perspectives. They operate often at a local level, are more radical in their outlook, are concerned with debates about representation and social justice, use different distribution mechanisms (especially now digital media), have flatter organizational structures, and try to achieve more democratic practices of production.[1] In this characterization, we have begun to connect alternative media with the various political and democratic discourses that continue to 'provide theoretical and intellectual support for their identities and practices' (Bailey et al. 2008: 4).

Of course, this presentation of alternative and mainstream media as distinct and dichotomous is overly simplistic (Pickard 2007). As many scholars have pointed out, referencing Downing (2001), everything is alternative to something else, and any form of media might be considered radical at some stage whether now or in the future; there is thus a diachronic perspective to all of this. As we have seen with regard to the fluidity of the media landscape, 'today's alternative may be co-opted and re-appropriated to become tomorrow's mainstream' (Pickard 2007). It can also be concluded that the 'ideological dimension' of alternative media is not easy to unpack (Pickard 2007). It is rather tempting to associate alternative media with left-leaning and even anarchic political interventions, but we should be live to the fact that alternative media are very often a conduit for conservative voices also. As has been said, it is also pertinent to question the rhetorics of democracy that accompany debate about alternative media. Such media might (in theory) open up the opportunities available for representation, but that does not in itself ensure parity or voice. As Christian Fuchs reminds us, 'a pluralistic media landscape, in which each consumer can become a media producer with the help of alternative media, is not automatically a media democracy' (Fuchs 2010: 178 see also Sandoval and Fuchs 2010).

In the following sections, two varied takes on alternative media will be examined; culture jamming (including yarnbombing) and the work of street artist Banksy. I will re-visit Fiske's concepts of 'incorporation' and 'containment' to demonstrate that, as Bailey et al. state, alternative media is 'important but vulnerable' (Bailey et al. 2008: 30). I have avoided concentrating here on initiatives such as Indymedia[2] or satirical papers such as *The Onion* or *The Daily Mash* because they have been written about extensively elsewhere. Instead, I focus on more ambiguous examples that help us explore alternative media's frustrated agency.

CULTURE JAMMING

One strand of alternative media output that has become instantly recognizable to many is subvertising, often also called brand jacking or culture jamming. Here, advertisements produced by corporations large and small are hacked in order to change the meaning of the signs and discourses at play therein; taking a marketing approach and 'exaggerating its tropes' so that it might present a completely oppositional message (Harold 2004: 189). Large global brands such as Coca Cola, McDonalds, Nike and Starbucks are seen as 'fair game' for those who are interested in critiquing the pervasiveness of commercial messages within society, and the dominant capitalist ideology that underpins their operations. Culture jammers seek to comment on the fact that brand messages have become so normalized we invariably fail to critically engage with them.

According to Graham Meikle, 'Culture jamming is the practice of taking familiar signs and trying to transform them into question marks' or even 'stop signs' (Meikle 2007: 167–168), and in so doing, attempting to expose, critique, and hold up to ridicule the means by which we are dominated. The practice 'turns corporate power against itself by co-opting, hacking, mocking, and re-contextualizing meanings' (Peretti and Micheletti 2006: 128). In the range of brand jacking examples that can be found by doing a simple online search we can see that, semiotically, these interventions can be very interesting indeed to our study of representations. We can utilize our knowledge of semiotics and branding to see how, in re-configuring a logo (say), myths and ideologies are exposed, questioned, and potentially even replaced by other logics. Culture jamming is 'about the manipulation and (re-)creation of existing cultural images in a way that results in images with a decidedly different, alternative message' (Coyer et al. 2007: 164).

A number of examples can be found on the website www. abrupt.org in the 'Culture jamming' section featuring their work. Two of the examples presented are parodies of adverts for four-by-four vehicles and feature familiar images of cars in natural (but extreme) locations – one a desert, the other arctic – as if in a traditional advertising campaign. The text of one reads 'Catastrophic Climate Change. Not Our Fault', the text of the other 'Nature. It'll Grow Back'. In these examples, all of the tropes of car advertisements are utilized to perform a critique. In the latter example the car is pictured in movement; dynamic, forceful. It tears up the surface upon which it travels presumably at speed. The environment within which the car is pictured is expansive, cinematic. These 'gas guzzling' cars are of course much-derided symbols in the fight against climate change. The text reads as a linguistic shrug of the shoulders, an attempt to replicate the standpoint of those who laugh in the face of the evidence to the contrary. Here, the sign systems, typographies, image choices, mise-en-scene, setting and lighting all replicate those found in traditional car adverts, but the message is flipped quite comprehensively by the text that anchors the image.

In another example from Adbusters, the torso of a naked man can be seen in close-up. We can assume it is a man from the hair comprehensively covering his chest. His is not the physique normally found in advertisements; not only is he hairy, but his body lacks definition. The photo is in black and white, the man is posing, it echoes the assemblage of signs found in perfume adverts. Yet the text reads 'REALITY for men' by 'Calvin Klien' (sic).

Another shows an expansive image of a cemetery. The grass is well tended, and the graves stand in rows as far as the eye can see. There are hundreds of them. 'Welcome to Marlboro Country' says the text echoing the slogan of the famous Marlboro tobacco adverts which began with 'Marlboro Man' in the 1950s.[3]

As these examples demonstrate, brand jacking uses as its start point, or its canvas, the source materials already available within culture (as with Fiske's jeans). Hackers use the same avenues for communication used by large corporations and politicians, but subvert their messages; seeking to expose the cracks in our culture by utilizing that very culture. As Meikle notes: 'most often jamming is self-reflexive media activism, in that it uses the media to address a media issue (the influence of advertising, for example)' (Meikle 2007: 167).

We might consider the examples *more* impactful for using approximations of the original adverts and even their typographies, than had they created a critique afresh in a different medium; an informational pamphlet for example. There is playfulness in the idea that you might (on first glance at least) not even notice the tampering of the jammer. This is then a form of 'DIY mischief-making' (Coyer et al. 2007: 163) or 'pranking' (Wettergren 2009). The lexical choice 'jamming' is worthy of examination here. According to Christine Harold, 'jamming' references the disruption of transmissions within CB radio culture (2004: 192), much like the jam in a traffic jam; a stoppage, a blockage, an interference. But it also has a musical referent; to jam is to playfully collaborate and experiment (Meikle 2007). What emerges very powerfully is that this is a form with playfulness at its core: significantly, for Åsa Wettergren; 'fun and pleasure in culture jamming are positioned as "real" emotions in contrast to the "fake" fun of consumer culture' (2009: 4–5).

The practice at the heart of culture jamming is not new, but is said to be founded in the French Situationists movement of the 1950s. The strategy of *detournement* (meaning turning around or upside down) was one where images were lifted from the original context and re-set in another that was seen to be more desirable. Two of the leading situationists, Guy Debord and Gil J. Wolman wrote in 1956 that 'Any sign or word is susceptible to being converted into something else, even into its opposite' (Debord and Wolman 1956: 13). This is very clearly what we see attempted in the examples above; an 'altering' of the 'fragments' (ibid.), forms of 'guerrilla semiotics' (Dery 2010) which specialize in sabotage.

The network that has become best known for their creation and circulation of such messages is the Adbusters Media Foundation, a Canadian organization founded in 1989 by Kalle Lasn. Its most notable outputs include the Adbusters magazine, and a number of campaigns including the International Buy Nothing Day held every November. Kalle Lasn says of the Adbusters 'mission':

> We call ourselves culture jammers. We're a loose global network of media activists who see ourselves as the advance shock troops of the most significant social movement of the next twenty years... it will change the way we interact with the mass media and the way in which meaning is produced in our society.
>
> (Lasn 2000: xi)

At its core is an anti-consumerist, anti-capitalist and (broadly) anti-American agenda. Adbusters understands mainstream culture as top-down and uninterested in the variety of human experience, the earth as unable to support our continued patterns of consumption, and America as a brand rather than a country; one that is leading us down the road to a global monoculture (Lasn 2000). The media are appointed the principal enemies in all of this, seen as dispensing damaging images, myths, promises and ideologies, and failing to question them or provide alternative messages and voices (a critique we have revisited variously throughout this book). If readers have never looked at a copy of Adbusters (or their website) I urge them to do so. For the study of representation, and of semiotics, it is a fascinating resource, and is not insignificant in terms of reach, having a paid circulation of about 60,000 in 2015 (Adbusters 2015). However, it might be noted that given the immensity and ubiquity of its target – consumer capitalism – it perhaps has limited scope for success in changing in any sustained way our relationship with mainstream media: James Carey calls it nothing more than 'a flea on the butt of capitalism' (Carey 2006: 256).

There are other forms of culture jamming which we might note here as of interest. One trend on the rise in many Western contexts is yarnbombing, examples of which can be found with an online search.[4] Here we see how such activities can be aligned with the maker movement; the increased interest and investment by 'ordinary people' in craft that is demonstrated in the wider societal growth in knitting groups, sewing bees, grow your own and artisan baking (Gauntlett 2011, Sennett 2008).[5] Danish artist Marianne Jørgensen's Pink M.24 Chaffee Tank was a fascinating case study of this practice that sees everyday objects and urban environments re-scripted through 'guerrilla knitting'. In this example, a full size tank was covered in a hot pink knitted and crocheted blanket in a protest at Denmark's involvement in the 2003 Iraq war. To top it off a single pink pom pom hung from the tank's canon. Here Jørgensen comprehensively 'jams' the original meaning of the text (the tank). A tank is cold, cumbersome and murderous, and those traits are only amplified and given renewed recognition in its re-interpretion as soft, warm, homely and impotent. We are forced to re-visit our idea of a tank and to see it a-fresh. Guerrilla gardening is another example of how the everyday is being freshly interpreted. Here, disused public spaces in urban landscapes are brought to life through being greened, and are often even brought into productivity; becoming host to vegetables or grains that might (at least symbolically) feed a community. Guerrilla gardening offers a commentary on our uses of public space and our social and environmental responsibility. It visits a twisted and sometimes jarring aesthetic on the everyday places of our lives and asks questions about our relationships to home, shelter, productivity and the cosmopolitan.

We see that in the practices of 'jamming', cultural texts are opened up for re-evaluation and interpretation in often surprising, and sometimes radical, ways. This reminds us again that sign systems are not static but – always and inevitably – subject to literal and metaphorical tearings. In acknowledging this point, Harold says the following:

> it may be more useful to consider jamming as an artful proliferation of messages, a rhetorical process of intervention and invention, which challenges the ability of corporate discourses to make meaning in predictable ways.

> (Harold 2004: 192)

However, as we will begin to see in the following section, these practices are often picked up by mainstream media and institutionalized in ways that are often only too predictable.

INSTITUTIONAL RESPONSES

> Manufacturers quickly exploited the popularity of ragged (or old or faded) jeans by producing factory-made tears, or by "washing" or fading jeans in the factory before sale ... adopting the signs of resistance incorporates them into the dominant system and thus attempts to rob them of any oppositional meaning.
>
> (Fiske 1990: 15–18)

The radical potential of jeans as a cultural resource for user-creativity was, as we saw in the opening section, soon recognized and nullified by the manufacturers themselves as they began to sell their own versions of ripped and dyed jeans. In so doing 'the raggedness of worn-out jeans, far from opposing consumerism, [was] turned into a way of extending and enhancing it' (Fiske 1990: 18). Their radical potential was suppressed through both *incorporation* into and *containment* within the mainstream. We have seen this in relation to the examples previously used in this chapter; many advertising campaigns now pre-empt the kind of user-creativity and parody that has been highlighted here. It is commonplace for producers of cultural goods, and their marketing and PR people, to have direct conversations with consumers; encouraging them to re-use or extend a brand using their own creative impulses, to share the outcomes within and across their various networks. Campaigns build in opportunities for participation and user-engagement, and even to poke fun. Food spread maker Marmite for example (a Unilever product), now embraces the love it/hate it dichotomy that originally came from user responses, and embraces it in their 'Love it or Hate it' campaign. In 2010 Unilever threatened the British National Party (a far-right political party in the UK) with legal action for trying to use their image and this slogan within their own campaign materials because the brand association made them distinctly uncomfortable (Jeffrey 2010).

There are other examples of organizations that have embraced the aesthetic and playfulness of the culture jamming approach. The California Department of Public Health anti-smoking campaign poster shown in Figure 6.2 is a case in point. The image is virtually indistinguishable from something that might have been produced by culture jammers, and cleverly works with the same principles.

Another example is in the embrace of flashmobbing by telephone company T-mobile in the UK. Flashmobs are public assemblages of groups of people to carry out some kind of deed or performative act – such as the No Pants Subway Ride or a dance – to be filmed and disseminated often via social media outlets. These activities emerged in the early 2000s and by 2007 were beginning to receive media coverage and interest. In 2009 T-Mobile launched their 'Dance' campaign with an advertisement filmed in Liverpool Street Station in London. 350 dancers came together to do a synchronized dance which was filmed by

Figure 6.2 Miss My Lung. Image courtesy of the California Department of Public Health, California Tobacco Control Program

hidden cameras – as were the unsuspecting commuters' responses. The campaign, which had been imagineered by Saatchi and Saatchi no less, invited members of the public to produce their own versions of the dance and to share them in response. The advert won the 'TV Commercial of the Year' award at the British television Advertising Awards that year. The follow-up, filmed in Trafalgar Square, was attended by more than 13,000 participants, and even featured the American singer Pink who was keen to get people singing along to her latest single release. At this point it seemed to many that flashmobbing had lost any innovative edge it might have had and become little more than a viral marketing stunt (Hargrave 2009).

Meikle says of such practices that they demonstrate 'the recuperation of resistance' (2007: 172) and Harold asserts that a major limitation of [say] Adbuster's reliance on parody as a reve-latory device is that this device has been enthusiastically embraced by marketers as well (Harold 2004: 192); taking radical ideas and co-opting them, absorbing them, appropriating them, defusing them, twisting them, and even commodifying them. Not only do such activities complicate the semiotic terrain yet again, but they raise questions about exploitation of participants for commercial gain. As Carducci summarizes:

> That so-called oppositional or 'counter' culture can quickly be recuperated by commercial interests and integrated back into the market system is another often-explored notion.
>
> (Carducci 2006: 118)

Carducci goes on to assert that we have found ourselves in a 'postmodern consumer paradigm' where 'rebellious expressive individualism' is accommodated 'as a matter of course' (2006: 123). Indeed, within that landscape, and with outputs like the Adbusters magazine itself, brand jackers themselves run the risk of becoming a 'brand community' (Carducci 2006: 124).

At this point I would like also to bring in the work of British street artist Banksy, and its arguable absorption into the main-stream. Echoing the discussion in Chapter 5 I take his commentary on museums as a start point, most specifically his practice in the mid-2000s of smuggling his own artworks into art galleries and hanging them amongst the paintings; at the British Museum (London), the Metropolitan Museum of Art (New York) and Tate Britain (London) perhaps most famously (BBC News 2005). In so doing Banksy vividly demonstrated that only certain kinds of art are legitimized within museum spaces whilst others are silently excluded, and asked uncomfortable questions about how cultural value is ascribed, who owns culture, and who gets to access it. Asked why he carried out the pranks, Bansky said, simply: 'I thought some of [the paintings] were quite good. That's why I thought, you know, put them in a gallery. Otherwise, they would just sit at home and no one would see them' (Banksy quoted in Norris 2005) Banksy's interventions, and his response, can be easily characterized as playful just like many of the other examples explored in this chapter. Yet of course what happened in the longer term was that the various museums, on finding out they had been pranked, and on learning more about Banksy and his appeal, went on to accession his works into their collections; to take ownership of them, to treat them like the other artefacts and artworks in their care, and to essentially neutralize their radical potential. To return again to Fiske we might ask is this incorporation? Wanting to include his work, tell a different story, widen representation, open up the collection to more recent and popular practice? Or was it a way of containing the radical potential of Banksy? To *stop* him questioning and exploring the meaning-making practices of art galleries by bringing him into the fold, legitimizing and canonizing him? Again we are reminded how complex and fragile our systems of representation are, and how interconnected with wider cultural and political debates.

CONCLUSION

At the end of this book I encourage readers to reflect on the plurality of media practice that has been covered, and the range of tensions that have been highlighted. The study of representation is concerned with the simultanity of being and seeing, constructing and consuming, presence and absence, noise and silence. Once recognized, issues around representation percolate and re-surface, often with alarming regularity – sometimes the jaw drops a little, sometimes the heart breaks a little. The landscape has no doubt become both more complex and more interesting given the pervasiveness of digital media and their associated rhetorics. It is my contention that within that context representation becomes not less but more important as a site of study and critique. But it should be more than that, and as we have seen in this chapter, often is. Representation is a site of active political, cultural and social movement within which we are, each and every one of us, implicated. That remains a weighty and misunderstood responsibility. To echo once again Stuart Hall (1997: 343), what is actually at stake is our will and our capacity to *be more human* to one another.

NOTES

1 This is not unproblematic, there are still those who have the resources to participate and those that do not; not least those that can afford to partake in precarious and even 'self-exploitative' labour (Sandoval and Fuchs 2010: 143).

2 Indymedia's practices are also now used by 'mainstream' news organizations such as *The Guardian*. We might question whether this is incorporation or containment of the activities at the heart of Indymedia and other groups like it.

3 The image is circulated widely online, yet I cannot find a credit.

4 Permissions for the re-production of images were difficult to secure for many of the examples used in this chapter. One explanation for this is the commercial nature of (much of) the publishing industry, thus making this publication out of step with the philosophy of most activity in this area.

5 This is a trend that is reflected in television output in the United Kingdom; *The Great British Bake Off* (2010–), *The Big Allotment Challenge* (2014–), *The Great British Sewing Bee* (2013–).

BIBLIOGRAPHY

Adbusters, 2015, 'About' page at https://www.adbusters.org/about/adbusters [Accessed 8th May 2015].

Adorno, Theodor, 1951 (1967), *Prisms: Cultural Criticism and Society*. London: Neville Spearman.

Allen, Kim and Mendick, Heather, 2012. 'Keeping it Real? Social Class, Young People and Authenticity in Reality TV', in *Sociology* online, first pp.1–17.

Albertazzi, Daniele and Cobley, Paul (eds), 2009, *The Media: An Introduction* (3rd Edition). Oxon and New York: Routledge.

Andrejevic, Mark, 2004, *Reality TV: The Work of Being Watched*. Oxford: Rowman and Littlefield.

Archibald, David, 2011, 'Photography, the Police and Protest Images of the G20, London 2009', in Cottle, Simon and Lester, Libby (eds), *Transnational Protests and the Media*. Oxford: Peter Lang, pp. 129–140.

Atton, Chris, 2002, *Alternative Media*. London: Sage.

Austin, J., 1962, *How to Do Things with Words*. Oxford: Clarendon.

Bailey, Olga Guedes, Cammaerts, Bart, and Carpentier, Nico, 2008, *Understanding Alternative Media*. New York and Berkshire: Open University Press.

Barbour, Kim, Marshall, P. David, and Moore, Christopher, 2014, 'Persona to Persona Studies', in *M/C Journal*, 17(3). Available at http://journal.media-culture.org.au/index.php/mcjournal/article/viewArticle/841/0 [Accessed 13th July 2015].

Barker, Chris, 2012, *Cultural Studies: Theory and Practice*. London, CA, New Delhi, Singapore: SAGE.

Barthes, Roland, 1957 (1972), *Mythologies*. New York: Noonday Press.

Barthes, Roland, 1977, *Image – Music – Text. Essays selected and translated [from the French] by Stephen Heath*. London: Fontana Press.

Bartlett, Jamie, Norrie, Richard, Patel, Sofia, Rumpel, Rebekka, and Wibberley, Simon, 2014, 'Misogyny on Twitter' published by DEMOS, London. Available at http://www.demos.co.uk/files/MISOGYNY_ON_TWITTER.pdf?1399567516 [Accessed 12th February 2015].

Baudrillard, Jean, 1995, *The Gulf War Did Not Take Place*. Indiana: Indiana University Press.

Baym, Nancy K., 2010, *Social Connections in the Digital Age*. Cambridge, UK and Malden, MA: Polity Press.

BBC News, 2015a, 'Equador President Rafael Correa's Troll Warfare', 30th January 2015. Available at http://www.bbc.co.uk/news/blogs-trending-31057933 [Accessed January 2015]

BBC News, 2015b, 'China Cracks Down on "Vulgar Culture" of Web Pseudonyms', 4th February 2015. Available at http://www.bbc.co.uk/news/world-asia-31127920 [Accessed April 2015].

BBC News, 2015c, 'Austrian Gay Couple Kiss Ban Sparks Café Prueckel Protest', 17th January 2015. Available at http://www.bbc.com/news/world-europe-30859791 [Accessed 10th May 2015].

BBC News, 2015d, 'Angolan TV Producers Apologise Over Gays Kissing', 4th February 2015. Available at http://www.bbc.com/news/world-africa-31128863 [Accessed 10th May 2015].

BBC News, 2013, 'David Cameron Defends Kate over Mantel Comments'. Available at http://www.bbc.co.uk/news/entertainment-arts-21502937 [Accessed 15th February 2015].

BBC News, 2005, 'Cave Art Hoax Hits British Museum'. Available at http://news.bbc.co.uk/2/hi/entertainment/4563751.stm [Accessed 8th May 2015].

BBC Newsbeat, 2014, 'Church Cancels Funeral Over Photos of Two Women "Overtly Kissing"', 14th January 2015. Available at http://www.bbc.co.uk/newsbeat/article/30814793/church-cancels-funeral-over-photos-of-two-women-overtly-kissing [Accessed 8th May 2015].

Benjamin, Walter, 1940, *On the Concept of History*. Available at http://www.sfu.ca/~andrewf/CONCEPT2.html [Accessed March 2015].

Benjamin, Walter, 1955 (1992 edition), *Illuminations*. Edited with an introduction by Hannah Arendt; translated by Harry Zohn. London: Fontana.

Bennett, Tony. 1995. *The Birth of the Museum: History Theory Politics*. London and New York: Routledge.

Bignell, Jonathon, 1997. *Media Semiotics: An Introduction*. Manchester and New York: Manchester University Press.

Biressi, Anita and Nunn, Heather, 2005, *Reality TV: Realism and Revelation*. New York and West Sussex: Wallflower Press.

Bourdieu, P., 1986, 'The Forms of Capital', in Richardson, J. (ed.), *Handbook of Theory and Research for the Sociology of Education*. New York: Greenwood.

Bowman, Paul, 2012, *Culture and the Media*. Hampshire: Palgrave Macmillan.

boyd, danah, 2007, 'Why Youth (Heart) Social Network Sites: The Role of Networked Publics in Teenage Social Life', in Buckingham, David (ed.), *Youth Identity and Digital Media*. Cambridge, MA: MIT Press.

boyd, danah, 2014, *It's Complicated: The Social Lives of Networked Teens*. New Haven and London: Yale University Press.

boyd, danah, Golder, Scott and Lotan, Gilad, 2010, 'Tweet, Tweet, Retweet: Conversational Aspects of Retweeting on Twitter', HICSS-43. IEEE: Kauai, HI, 6th January.

Boym, Svetlana, 2001, *The Future of Nostalgia*. New York: Basic Books.

Branston, Gill and Stafford, Roy, 2010, *The Media Student's Book* (5th Edition). Oxon and New York: Routledge.

Brenton, Sam and Cohen, Reuben, 2003, *Shooting People: Adventures in Reality TV*. London and New York: Verso.

Brown, Mark, 2013, 'Kate Speech, Hate Speech and Hilary Mantel's Dissection of Royal Bodies', in *The Guardian*, 19th February 2013. Available at http://www.theguardian.com/uk/2013/feb/19/kate-hilary-mantel-duchess-cambridge [Accessed March 2015].

Brown, Mark, 2014, 'Blood-swept Lands: The Story behind the Tower of London Poppies Tribute', *The Guardian*, Sunday, 28 December 2014. Available at http://www.theguardian.com/world/2014/dec/28/blood-swept-lands-story-behind-tower-of-london-poppies-first-world-war-memorial [Accessed 14th January 2015].

Budweiser, 2015, 'Dream Goal: Send Us Your Screamers'. Available at http://www.budweiser.co.uk/DreamGoal?gclid=CjoKEQjwpM2pBRChsZCzm_CUot4BEi-QAxDVFmjisegINtU2FeoiVpmLgS1NJK6Gg4NPiivBi6uaE7FoaAqiv8P8HAQ [Accessed 15th April 2015].

Burchill, Julie, 2013, 'Here is Julie Burchill's Censored Observer Article', re-produced via Toby Young. *The Telegraph*, 14th January 2013. Available at http://blogs.telegraph.co.uk/news/tobyyoung/100198116/here-is-julie-burchills-censored-observer-article [Accessed January 2015].

Burgess, Jean and Green, Joshua, 2009, *YouTube: Online Video and Participatory Culture*. Cambridge, UK and Malden, MA: Polity Press.

Burton, Christine and Scott, Carol, 2003, 'Museums: Challenges for the 21st Century', in *International Journal of Arts Management*, 5(2): 56.

Cameron, F. and Kelly, L. (eds), 2010, *Hot Topics, Public Culture, Museums*. Newcastle: Cambridge Scholars.

Cannadine, David, 2004, *History and the Media*. Basingstoke: Palgrave.

Carducci, Vince, 2006, 'Culture Jamming: A Sociological Perspective', in *Journal of Consumer Culture*, 6(1): 116–138.

Carey, James, 2006, 'A Review of "Culture Jam: Hijacking Commercial Culture"', in *Political Communication*, 22(2): 255–257.

Chandler, Daniel, 2014, *Semiotics for Beginners*. Available at http://visual-memory.co.uk/daniel/Documents/S4B [Accessed 8th May 2015].

Charles, Alec, 2012, *Interactivity: New Media, Politics and Society*. Oxford: Peter Lang.

Cheney-Rice, Zak, 2014, '16 Stunning Photos That Shatter Society's Stereotypes About Asian Men', 17th November 2014. Available at http://mic.com/articles/104332/16-stunning-images-shatter-stereotypes-about-asian-men [Accessed 25th March 2015].

Cook, Guy, 2001, *The Discourse of Advertising* (2nd edition). London and New York: Routledge.

Coyer, Kate, Dowmunt, Tony, and Fountain, Alan, 2007, *The Alternative Media Handbook*. London and New York: Routledge.

Corner, John, 2000, 'What Can we Say About "Documentary"?' *Media, Culture and Society*, 22(5): 681–688.

Corner, John, 2002, 'Performing the Real: Documentary Diversions', in *Television and New Media*, 3(3): 255–269.

Couldry, Nick, 2012, *Media, Society, World: Social Theory and Digital Media Practice*. Cambridge, UK and Malden, MA: Polity Press.

Couldry, Nick, 2006, 'Media and the Ethics of "Reality" Construction', in *Southern Review: Communication, Politics & Culture*, 39(1): 42–53.

Couldry, Nick and Littler, Jo, 2008, 'The Work of Work: Reality TV and the Negotiation of Neoliberal Labour in *The Apprentice*', in Austin, Thomas and de Jong,

Wilma (eds), *Rethinking Documentary: New Perspectives and Practices.* Maidenhead: Open University Press, pp. 258–267.

Cuno, James, 2014, 'Culture War: The Case Against Repatriating Museum Artifacts', in *Foreign Affairs*, November/December 2014 issue. Available at http://www. foreignaffairs.com/articles/142185/james-cuno/culture-war [Accessed April 2015].

Cushion, Stephen, Moore, Kerry, and Jewell, John, 2011, 'Media Representations of Black Young Men and Boys', report of the REACH media monitoring project, London: Department of Communities and Local Government. Available at http://lx.iriss.org.uk/sites/default/files/resources/2113275.pdf [Accessed 4th February 2015].

Danesi, Marcel, 2008, 'The Medium is the Sign: Was McLuhan a Semiotician?' in *MediaTropes*, 1: 113–126.

Danesi, Marcel, 2002, *Understanding Media Semiotics.* London: Arnold.

De Groot, Jerome, 2011, 'Downton Abbey: Nostalgia For An Idealised Past?' in *History Today*, 19th September 2011. Available at http://www.historytoday.com/blog/2011/09/downton-abbey-nostalgia-idealised-past [Accessed February 2015].

Debord, Guy, 1967 (2006), *The Society of the Spectacle.* London: Rebel Press.

Debord, Guy and Wolman, Gil J., 1956, *A User's Guide to Détournement.* Available at http://www.bopsecrets.org/SI/detourn.htm [Accessed 8th July 2015].

Deery, June, 2015, *Reality TV.* Cambridge, UK and Malden, MA: Polity Press.

Derrida, Jacques, 1967 (2005 edition with 1978 translation), *Writing and Difference.* London: Routledge.

Dery, Mark, 2010, Culture Jamming: Hacking, Slashing, and Sniping in the Empire of Signs. Introduction to the reprint. Available at http://markdery.com/?page_id=154 [Accessed 9th April 2015].

Devereux, Eoin, 2007, *Understanding the Media* (3rd Edition, 2014). London, California, New Delhi and Singapore: SAGE.

Dicks, Bella, 2003, *Culture on Display: The Production of Contemporary Visitability.* Berkshire: Open University Press.

Dodge, Shyam, 2015, 'How Much Did Caitlyn Jenner's New Face Cost? Six Surgeries and $70,000 Says One Doctor', in *Daily Mail*, 4th June 2015. Available at http://www.dailymail.co.uk/tvshowbiz/article-3111436/Caitlyn-Jenner-six-sur-geries-spent-70-000-new-face-says-one-doctor.html [Accessed 5th June 2015].

Dowmunt, Tony (with Coyer, Kate), 2007, 'Introduction', to Coyer, Kate, Dowmunt, Tony, and Fountain, Alan, *The Alternative Media Handbook.* London and New York: Routledge, pp. 1–12.

Downing, John D. H., 1988, 'The Alternative Public Realm: The Organization of the 1980s Anti-nuclear Press in Germany and Britain', in *Media, Culture and Society*, 10(2): 163–181.

Downing, John D. H. with Ford, Tamara Villarreal, Gil, Geneve and Stein, Laura, 2001, *Radical Media: Rebellious Communication and Social Movements.* London: Sage.

The Economist, 2013, 'Mad about Museums'. Available at http://www.economist.com/news/special-report/21591710-china-building-thousands-new-museums-how-will-it-fill-them-mad-about-museums [Accessed 27th April 2015].

Ellison, Nicole, Heino, Rebecca, and Gibbs, Jennifer, 2006, 'Managing Impressions Online: Self-Presentation Processes in the Online Dating Environment', in *Journal of Computer-Mediated Communication*, 11(2): 415–441.

Enli, G. S. and Thumim, N., 2012, 'Socialising and Self Representation Online: Exploring Facebook', *Observatorio* (OBS), 6(1): 87–105.

Evans, Stephen, 2015, 'The Koreans Who Televise Themselves Eating Dinner', 5th February 2015. Available at http://www.bbc.co.uk/news/magazine-31130947 [Accessed March 2015].

Facebook, 2012, 'Chairs are Like Facebook Advert', produced by Wieden and Kennedy. Available at https://www.youtube.com/watch?v=SSzoDPptYNA [Accessed 8th July 2015].

Facebook, 2015, 'Statement of Rights and Responsibilities'. Available at https://www.facebook.com/legal/terms [Accessed March 2015].

Fairclough, N., 2010, *Critical Discourse Analysis: The Critical Study of Language*. Oxon and New York: Routledge.

Fenton, Natalie, 2012, 'The Internet and Social Networking', in Curran, James, Fenton, Natalie, and Freedman, Des, *Misunderstanding the Internet*. Oxon and New York: Routledge, pp. 121–148.

Fiore, Andrew T., 2008, 'Self-presentation and Deception in Online Dating', paper to CHE 2008, Florence Italy. Available at http://people.ischool.berkeley.edu/~atf/papers/fiore_secrets_lies.pdf [Accessed February 2015].

Fiske, John, 1990, *Understanding Popular Culture* (2nd Edition). London and New York: Routledge.

Fivusch, Robyn, 2010, 'Speaking Silence: The Social Construction of Silence in Autobiographical and Cultural Narratives', in *Memory* 18(2): 88–98.

Fowler, Roger, 1991, *Language in the News: Discourse and Ideology in the Press*. London: Routledge.

Foucault, Michel, 1981 (1990), *The History of Sexuality*. New York and Toronto: Vintage Books, Random House.

Foucault, Michel, 1980, *Power/Knowledge: Selected Interviews and Other Writings 1972–1977* (ed. by Colin Gordon). New York: Pantheon Books.

Foucault, Michel, 1979 (1995), *Discipline and Punish: The Birth of the Prison*. New York and Toronto: Vintage Books, Random House.

Foucault, Michel, 1969 (2008), *Archaeology of Knowledge*. Oxon: Routledge.

Fuchs, Christian, 2014, *Social Media: A Critical Introduction*. CA and London: SAGE.

Fuchs, Christian, 2010, 'Alternative Media as Critical Media', in *European Journal of Social Theory*, 13(2): 173–192.

Furness, Hannah, 2013, 'Hilary Mantel Portrays Duchess of Cambridge as a "Shop Window Mannequin"', in *The Telegraph*, 18th February 2013. Available at http://www.telegraph.co.uk/news/uknews/kate-middleton/9878818/Hilary-Mantel-portrays-Duchess-of-Cambridge-as-a-shop-window-mannequin.html [Accessed January 2015].

Garde-Hansen, Joanne, 2011, *Media and Memory*. Edinburgh: Edinburgh University Press.

Gere, Charlie, 2008, *Digital Culture* (2nd Edition). London: Reaktion Books.

Gill, Rosalind, 2007, *Gender and the Media*. Cambridge, UK and Malden, MA: Polity Press.

Glassberg, David, 1986, 'Living in the Past', in *American Quarterly*, 38(2) (Summer): 305–310.

Glynn, Kevin, 2000, *Tabloid Culture: Trash Taste, Popular Power, and the Transformation of American Television*. Durham, NC and London: Duke University Press.

Goffman, Erving, 1956, *The Presentation of Self in Everyday Life*. Edinburgh: University of Edinburgh Social Sciences Research Centre.

Gomes, R. C. and Williams, L. F., 1990, 'Race and Crime: The Role of the Media in Perpetuating Racism and Classism in America', in *Urban League Review*, 14(1): 57–70.

Gordon, Bryony, 2015, 'As We Proclaim "Je Suis Charlie" – What About the Victims Twitter Forgot?', in *The Telegraph*, 13th January 2015. Available at http://www.telegraph.co.uk/news/worldnews/europe/france/11340478/As-we-all-proclaim-Je-Suis-Charlie-what-about-the-victims-Twitter-forgot.html [Accessed February 2015].

Gray, Ann and Bell, Erin, 2013, *History on Television*. Oxon and New York: Routledge.

Grindstaff, Laura and Murray, Susan, 2015, 'Reality Celebrity: Branded Affect and the Emotion Economy', in *Public Culture*, 27(1): 109–135.

Gripsrud, Jostein, 2006, 'Semiotic: Signs, Codes and Cultures' (adapted by Jason Toynbee and Davud Hesmondhalgh), in Gillespie, Marie and Toynbee, Jason (eds), 2006, *Analysing Media Texts*. New York: McGraw Hill, pp. 9–42.

Habermas, Jurgen, 1994, *The Polity Reader in Cultural Theory*. Cambridge: Polity Press in association with Blackwell.

Hall, Stuart, Evans, Jessica, and Nixon, Sean (eds), 2013, *Representation* (2nd Edition). Milton Keynes: Open University.

Hall, Stuart (ed.), 1997, *Representation: Cultural Representations and Signifying Practices*. Milton Keynes: Open University.

Hall, Stuart, 1982, 'The Rediscovery of Ideology: The Return of the Repressed in Media Study', in Gurevitch, M., Curran, J., Bennett, T. and Woollacott, J. (eds), *Culture, Society and the Media*. London: Methuen, pp. 52–86.

Hall, Stuart, 1973. *Encoding and Decoding in the Television Discourse*. Birmingham, England: Centre for Cultural Studies, University of Birmingham.

Hall, Stuart, 1980 (1973), 'Encoding/decoding', in Centre for Contemporary Cultural Studies (ed.), *Culture, Media, Language: Working Papers in Cultural Studies, 1972–79*. London: Hutchinson, pp. 128–138.

Hamilton, Trudy, 2015, 'What's Really Going On With The Sexist Backlash Against Selfies'. Available at http://www.gradientlair.com/post/115395306478/sexist-backlash-against-selfies#disqus_thread [Accessed 7th April 2015].

Hargrave, Steve, 2009, 'Singer Pink in London Flash Mob Ad Campaign'. Available at http://news.sky.com/story/688770/singer-pink-in-london-flash-mob-ad-campaign [Accessed 8th May 2015].

Harold, Christine, 2004, 'Pranking Rhetoric: "Culture Jamming" as Media Activism', in *Cultural Studies in Media Communication*, 21(3): 189–211.

Harris, Geraldine, 2006, *Beyond Representation: Television Drama and the Politics and Aesthetics of Identity*. Manchester and New York: Manchester University Press.

Hartley, John, 2012, *Digital Futures for Cultural and Media Studies*. West Sussex: Wiley-Blackwell.

Hartley, John, Potts, Jason, Cunningham, Stuart, Flew, Terry, Keane, Michael and Banks, John, 2012, *Key Concepts in Creative Industries*. London, California, New Delhi, Singapore: SAGE.

Hattenstone, Simon, 2013, 'Caroline Criado-Perez: "Twitter has Enabled People to Behave in a Way they Wouldn't Face to Face', 4 August 2013, in *The Guardian. Available at* http://www.theguardian.com/lifeandstyle/2013/aug/04/caroline-criado-perez-twitter-rape-threats [Accessed January 2015].

Hayward, Keith and Yar, Majid, 2006, 'The "Chav" Phenomenon: Consumption, Media and the Construction of a New Underclass', in *Crime, Media, Culture* 2 (1): 9–28 [Accessed December 2014].

Hearn, Alison, 2008, '"Meat, Mask, Burden": Probing the contours of the branded "self"', in the *Journal of Consumer Culture*, 8(2): 197–217.

Heil, Bill and Piskorski, Mikolaj, 2009, 'New Twitter Research: Men Follow Men and Nobody Tweets', 1st June 2009. Available at https://hbr.org/2009/06/new-twitter-research-men-follo [Accessed 12th April 2015].

Henning, Michelle, 2005, *Museums, Media and Cultural Theory* (Issues in Cultural and Media Studies). Berkshire, England: Open University Press.

Herman, David, 2013, 'Horlicks for Chummy: Britain's Romance with Cosy TV Nostalgia' in New Statesman 27th February 2013. Available at http://www.newstatesman.com/culture/culture/2013/02/horlicks-chummy-britain%E2%80%99s-romance-cosy-tv-nostalgia. [Accessed 12th February 2015].

Hill, Annette, 2015, *Reality TV*. Oxon and NY: Routledge.

Hill, Annette, 2005, *Reality TV Audiences and Popular Factual Television*. Oxon and New York: Routledge.

Hilsen, Anne Inga and Helvik, Tove, 2012, 'The Construction of Self in Social Medias, Such as Facebook', in *AI and Society*, 29(1): 3–10.

Hindman, Matthew, 2009, *The Myth of Digital Democracy*. NJ & Oxfordshire: Princeton University Press.

Hodges, Caroline, Jackson, Daniel, Scullion, Richard, Thompson, Shelley, and Molesworth, Mike, 2014, 'Tracking Changes in Everyday Experiences of Disability and Disability Sport within the Context of the 2012 London Paralympics', CMC Publishing: Bournemouth University. Available at https://microsites.bournemouth.ac.uk/cmc/files/2014/10/BU-2012-London-Paralympics.pdf [Accessed 2nd February 2015].

Hoggart, Richard, 1957, *The Uses of Literacy*. London: Penguin Books.

Holdsworth, Amy, 2011, *Television, Memory and Nostalgia*. Basingstoke: Palgrave Macmillan.

Holley, Peter, 2015, 'Teen Killed Classmate and Uploaded "Selfie" with the Body to Snapchat, Police Say', in *The Washington Post*, 8th February 2015. Available at http://www.washingtonpost.com/news/post-nation/wp/2015/02/08/teen-murdered-classmate-and-uploaded-selfie-with-the-body-to-snapchat-police-say [Accessed 8th July 2015].

Holmes, Su and Jermyn, Deborah (eds), 2004, *Understanding Reality Television*. London and New York: Routledge.

Holpuch, Amanda, 2014, 'Facebook Still Freezing Accounts Despite Apology to Drag Queens Over "Real Names"', in *The Guardian*, 7th October 2014. Available at http://www.theguardian.com/technology/2014/oct/17/facebook-still-freezing-accounts-despite-apology-drag-queens-real-names [Accessed January 2015].

Huffington Post, 2014, 'TV Host walks Off Set Over Michael Sam Kiss'. Available at http://www.huffingtonpost.com/2014/05/14/dallas-morning-anchor-michael-sam-tv_n_5324870.html [Accessed 8th July 2015].

Hunter, Dan, Lobato, Ramon, Richardson, Megan, and Thomas, Julian (eds), 2014, *Amateur Media: Social, Cultural and Legal Perspectives* (2nd Edition). Oxon and New York: Routledge.

Iles, Jennifer, 2008, 'In Remembrance: The Flanders Poppy', in *Mortality*, 13(3): 201–221.

Infante, Francesca, 2013, '"A Plastic Princess Designed to Breed": Bring Up the Bodies author Hilary Mantel's venomous attack on Kate Middleton', in *Mail Online*, 19th February 2013. Available at http://www.dailymail.co.uk/news/article-2280911/Duchess-Cambridge-plastic-princess-designed-breed-Booker-prize-winner-Hilary-Mantels-venomous-attack-Kate.html [Accessed January 2015].

internet.org, 2014, 'State of Connectivity: 2014 A Report on Global Internet Access'. Available at https://fbnewsroomus.files.wordpress.com/2015/02/state-of-connectivity1.pdf [Accessed February 2015].

Jackson, Daniel, Hodges, Caroline, Molesworth, Mike and Scullion, Richard (eds), 2014, *Reframing Disability? Media, (Dis)Empowerment and the Voice in the 2012 Paralympics*. New York and Oxon: Routledge.

Jeffers, Alison, 2011, *Refugees, Theatre and Crisis: Performing Global Identities*. Basingstoke: Palgrave Macmillan.

Jeffrey, Simon, 2010, 'Marmite and the BNP: Love Them or Hate Them, They've Added a New Taste to the Election'. Available at http://www.theguardian.com/politics/blog/2010/apr/22/general-election-20101 [Accessed 8th May 2015].

Jenkins, Henry, 2011, 'Transmedia 202: Further Reflections'. Available at http://henryjenkins.org/2011/08/defining_transmedia_further_re.html [Accessed 13th July 2013].

Jin, Gracie, 2013, 'Why 600 Million People Are Watching This Chinese Reality Show', 26th December 2013. Available at http://mic.com/articles/77427/why-600-million-people-are-watching-this-chinese-reality-show [Accessed March 2015].

Jones, Jonathan, 2014. 'The Tower of London Poppies are Fake, Trite and Inward-looking – A Ukip-style Memorial', *The Guardian*, Tuesday, 28 October 2014. Available at http://www.theguardian.com/artanddesign/jonathanjonesblog/2014/oct/28/tower-of-london-poppies-ukip-remembrance-day [Accessed 14th January 2015].

Jones, Owen, 2011, *Chavs: The Demonization of the Working Class*. London and New York: Verso.

Jorgensen, Marianne and Phillips, Louise J. 2002, *Discourse Analysis as Theory and Method*. London, CA, New Delhi: SAGE.

Joseph, Natasha and Blignaut, Charl, 2014, 'State versus Oscar Pistorius: A New Breed of Reality TV', for *City News*, 2nd March 2014. Available at http://www.citypress.co.za/news/state-versus-oscar-pistorius-new-breed-reality-tv [Accessed March 2015].

Kavka, Misha, 2012, *Reality TV*, Edinburgh: Edinburgh University Press.

Kelsey, Darren and Bennett, Lucy, 2014, 'Discipline and Resistance on Social Media: Discourse, Power and Context in the Paul Chambers "Twitter Joke Trial"', in *Discourse, Context and Media*, 3: 37–45.

Kendall, Geraldine, 2013, 'World View', in *Museums Journal*, 113(07):22–27.

Kershaw, Ian, 2004, 'The Past on the Box: Strengths and Weaknesses', in Cannadine, David, *History and the Media*. Basingstoke: Palgrave, pp. 118–123.

Kidd, Jenny, 2014, *Museums in the New Mediascape: Transmedia, Participation, Ethics*, Surrey: Ashgate.

Kidd, Jenny, Cairns, Samantha, Drago, Alex, Ryall, Amy and Stearn, Miranda (eds), 2014, *Challenging History in the Museum: International Perspectives*. Surrey: Ashgate.

Kirshenblatt-Gimblett, B. 1998. *Destination Culture: Tourism, Museums and Heritage*. Berkeley: University of California Press.

Knight, Megan, 2015, 'Data Journalism in the UK: A Preliminary Analysis of Form and Content', in *Journal of Media Practice*, 16(1): 55–72.

Kramer, Adam D. I., Guillory, Jamie E. and Hancock, Jeffrey T. 2014. 'Experimental Evidence of Massive-scale Emotional Contagion through Social Networks', in Proceedings of the National Academy of Sciences for the USA, 111(24). Available at http://www.pnas.org/content/111/24/8788.full [Accessed April 2015].

Kosinki, Michal, Stillwell, David, Graepel, Thore, 2013, 'Private Traits and Attributes are Predictable from Digital Records of Human Behavior', in *Proceedings of the National Academy of Sciences of the United States of America*, 110(15): 5802–5805.

Lasn, Kalle, 2000, *Culture Jam: How to Reverse America's Suicidal Consumer Binge – and Why We Must*. New York: Harper Collins.

Lester, Paul Martin, 2010, *Visual Communication: Images with Messages* (5th Edition). Boston, MA: Cengage Learning.

Lewis, Tim, 2014, 'Oscar Pistorius Trial Books Review – The Case that Mesmerised the World', in *The Guardian*, 23rd November 2014. Available at http://www.theguardian.com/books/2014/nov/23/oscar-pistorius-trial-books-review-june-steenkamp-john-carlin-barry-bateman [Accessed 8th July 2015].

Lidchi, Henrietta, 1997, 'The Poetics and the Politics of Exhibting Other Cultures', in Hall, Stuart (ed.), *Representation: Cultural Representations and Signifying Practices*. Milton Keynes: Open University.

Littlejohn, Richard, 2013, 'To Boldly Go Where No Man's Gone Before...', in *Mail Online*, 18th February 2013. Available at http://www.dailymail.co.uk/debate/article-2280745/To-boldly-mans-gone-.html [Accessed January 2015].

Lopez, Antonio, 2012, available at http://mediacology.com/2012/10/08/facebooks-mistaken-identity [Accessed 13th April 2015].

McGrath, John, 2004, *Loving Big Brother: Surveillance Culture and Performance Space*. London and New York: Routledge.

McLuhan, Marshall, 1964 (2005) *Understanding Media: The Extensions of Man*. London: Routledge.

McRobbie, Angela, 2004, 'Notes on "What Not To Wear" and Post-feminist Symbolic Violence', in *The Sociological Review*, 52(2): 97–109.

Machin, David and Mayr, Andrea, 2012, *How to Do Critical Discourse Analysis: A Multimodal Introduction*. London, CA, New Delhi and Singapore: SAGE.

Madrigal, Alexis C. 2015 'Many, Many Facebook Users Still Don't Know that their News Feeds are Filtered by an Algorithm', 27th March 2015. Available at http://fusion.net/story/110543/most-facebook-users-still-dont-know-that-their-news-feeds-are-filtered-by-an-algorithm [Accessed April 2015].

Mallan, Kerry and Giardina, Natasha, 2009, 'Wikidentities: Young People Collaborating on Virtual Identities in Social Network Sites', in *First Monday*, 14(6). Available at http://firstmonday.org/ojs/index.php/fm/article/view/2445/2213 [Accessed 19th April 2015].

Mandiberg, Michael, 2012 (ed.), *The Social Media Reader*. New York and London: New York University Press.

Manovich, Lev, 2010, available at http://www.datavisualisation.org/2010/11/lev-manovich-what-is-visualization [Accessed 13th July 2015].

Mantel, Hilary, 2013, 'Royal Bodies', in *London Review of Books*, 35(4): 3–7. Available at http://www.lrb.co.uk/v35/n04/hilary–mantel/royal–bodies [Accessed 22nd July 2015].

Marshall, P. David, 2014, 'Persona Studies: Mapping the Proliferation of the Public Self', in *Journalism*, 15(2): 153–170.

Marwick, Alice, 2014, *Status Update: Celebrity, Publicity, and Branding in the Social Media Age*. New Haven, CT: Yale University Press.

Marwick, Alice E. and boyd, danah, 2010, 'I Tweet Honestly, I Tweet Passionately: Twitter Users, Context Collapse, and the Imagined Audience', in *New Media and Society* 20(10): 1–20.

Marshall, P. David, 2006, *The Celebrity Culture Reader*. London: Routledge.

Mashhour, Hesham and Murphy, Com, 2014, 'All-male Abortion Debate at Oxford Cancelled', in *The Cambridge Student*, 18 November 2014. Available at http://www.tcs.cam.ac.uk/news/0033374-all-male-abortion-debate-at-oxford-cancelled.html [Accessed 27th Jan 2015].

McCosker, Anthony and Wilken, Rowan, 2014, 'Rethinking "Big Data" as Visual Knowledge: The Sublime and the Diagrammatic in Data Visualisation', in *Visual Studies*, 29(2): 155–164.

McCrae, John, 1915 (2012), *In Flanders Fields: And Other Poems of the First World War*. London: Arcturus Publishing Limited.

McNulty, Bernadette, 2013, 'Gogglebox: The TV Show Making Britain Feel Great', in *The Telegraph*, 11th December 2013. Available at http://www.telegraph.co.uk/

culture/tvandradio/10480336/Gogglebox-the-TV-show-making-Britain-feel-great. html [Accessed March 2015].

McQuail, Denis, 1984 *Communications*. Oxon and New York: Routledge.

Meikle, Graham, 2007, 'Stop Signs: An Introduction to Culture Jamming', in Coyer, Kate, Dowmunt, Tony, and Fountain, Alan, *The Alternative Media Handbook*. London and New York: Routledge.

Mercer, K. (1999) 'Reading Racial Fetishism', in Evans, J. and Hall, S. (eds), *Visual Culture: The Reader*. London: Sage/Open University, pp. 448–456.

Micheletti, Michele, Stolle, Dietland, and Follesdal, Andreas, 2006, *Politics, Products and Markets: Exploring Political Consumerism Past and Present*. New Jersey: Transaction Publishing.

Morey, Peter and Yaqin, Amina, 2011, *Framing Muslims: Stereotyping and Representation after 9/11*. Cambridge MA: Harvard University Press.

Morris, Regan, 2015, 'Transgender 13-year-old Zoey Having Therapy', 12th January 2015. Available at http://www.bbc.co.uk/news/world-us-canada-30783983 [Accessed January 2015].

Murray, S. and Ouellette, L., 2009, *Reality TV: Remaking Television Culture*. New York and London: New York University Press.

Naughton, John, 2012, *What You Really Need To Know About the Internet: From Gutenberg to Zuckerberg*. London: Quercus.

Negra, Diane, Pike, Kirsten, and Radley, Emma, 2012, 'Gender, Nation and Reality TV', in *Television and New Media*, 14(3): 187–193.

Nelson, Sara, 2015, 'Caitlyn Jenner Mocked and Misgendered by FoxNews Anchors Who Call Her Bruce', in *Huffington Post* (2nd June 2015). Available at http://www.huffingtonpost.co.uk/2015/06/02/caitlyn-jenner-mocked-misgendered-fox-news-anchors-bruce_n_7491452.html [Accessed 5th June 2015].

news.com.au, 2013, 'Reeva Steenkamp Leaves Haunting TV Show Message on Tropika Island of Treasure after Oscar Pistorius Faces Murder Charge'. Available at http://www.news.com.au/entertainment/tv/reeva-steenkamp-leaves-haunting-tv-show-message-on-tropika-island-of-treasure-after-oscar-pistorius-faces-murder-charge/story-e6frfmyi-1226579605579 [Accessed March 2015].

Nielsen, 2013, 'Tops of 2013: TV and Social Media', 17th December 2014. Available at http://www.nielsen.com/us/en/insights/news/2013/tops-of-2013-tv-and-social-media.html [Accessed March 2015].

Norris, Michele, 2005, '"Hang and Run" Artist Strikes NYC Museums'. Available at www.npr.org/templates/story/story.php?storyId=4559961 [Accessed 13th August 2015].

NPR, 2013, 'Laverne Cox: Transgender Actress on the Challenges of Her "New Black" Role', 7th August 2013. Available at http://www.npr.org/2013/08/07/209843353/orange-is-the-new-black-actress-calls-role-complicated [Accessed January 2015].

NUS, 2010, '1000 Candidates Sign Vote for Students Pledge to Oppose Tuition Fee Hike'. Available at http://www.nus.org.uk/en/news/lib-dem-and-labour-mps-would-vote-together-to-oppose-tuition-fee-rise, 26 April 2010 [Accessed 6th April 2015].

O'Reilly, Tim, 2005, 'What is Web 2.0?' Available at http://www.oreilly.com/pub/a/web2/archive/what-is-web-20.html [Accessed 3rd April 2015].

Ouellette, Laurie, 2010, 'Reality TV Gives Back: On the Civic Functions of Reality Entertainment', in *Journal of Popular Film and Television*, 38(2): 66–71.

Papacharissi, Zizi (ed), 2011, *A Networked Self: Identity, Community, and Culture on Social Network Sites*. New York and Oxon: Routledge.

Papacharissi, Zizi, 2002, 'The Presentation of Self in Virtual Life: Characteristics of Personal Homepages', in *Journalism and Mass Communication Quarterly*, 79(3): 643–660.

Parekh, Bhikhu, 2000, *The Future of Multi-Ethnic Britain*. London: Profile Books.

Paris, Michael (ed.), 2007, *Repicturing the Second World War: Representations in Film and Television*. Hampshire and New York: Palgrave Macmillan.

Peirce, Charles Sanders, 1894 (1998), *The Essential Peirce*. IN: Indiana University Press.

Peretti, Jonah with Micheletti, Michele, 2006, 'The Nike Sweatshop Email: Political Consumerism, Internet, and Culture Jamming', in Micheletti, Michele, Stolle, Dietland, and Follesdal, Andreas (eds), *Politics, Products and Markets: Exploring Political Consumerism Past and Present*. NJ: Transaction Publishers, pp. 127–142.

Philo, Greg (ed.), 1999, *Message Received*. New York: Longman.

Pickard, Victor W., 2007, 'Alternative Media', in Schaefer, Todd M. and Birkland, Thomas A. (eds), *The Encyclopaedia of Media an Politics*. Washington DC: CQ Press, pp. 12–13.

Prendergast, Christopher, 2000, *The Triangle of Representation*. New York and West Sussex: Columbia University Press.

Womack, Sarah, 2005, 'Puttnam Blames Violent Films for Increase in Playground Bullying', in The Telegraph, 20 April 2005. Available at http://www.telegraph. co.uk/news/uknews/1488224/Puttnam-blames-violent-films-for-increase-in-playground-bullying.html [Accessed 8th May 2015].

Raeside, Julia, 2011, 'A Different Kind of Reality TV', in *The Guardian*. Available at http://www.theguardian.com/tv-and-radio/2011/jun/01/reality-tv-only-way-essex [Accessed March 2015].

Reilly, Jill, 2013, 'Outrage at "Sick" Reeva Steenkamp Reality TV Show: Bosses Accused of Cashing in on Death of Blade Runner's Girlfriend as they Broad-cast Her 'Exit' Interview', in *The Daily Mail*, 18th February 2013. Available at http://www.dailymail.co.uk/news/article-2280400/Oscar-Pistorius-Outrage-Reeva-Steenkamps-reality-TV-exit-interview-aired.html#ixzz3VuEtAmOw [Accessed March 2015].

Retberg, Jill Walker, 2014, *Seeing Ourselves Through Technology: How We Use Selfies, Blogs and Wearable Devices to See and Shape Ourselves*. Hampshire and New York: Palgrave Macmillan.

Richardson, John E., 2007, *Analysing Newspapers: An Approach from Critical Discourse Analysis*. London: Palgrave Macmillan.

Riddle, Karyn and De Simone, J. J., 2013, 'A Snooki Effect? An Exploration of the Surveillance Subgenre of Reality TV and Viewers' Beliefs About the "Real" Real World', in *Psychology of Popular Media Culture*, 2(4): 237–250.

Ridley, Louise, 2015, 'Andreas Lubitz "Depression" Headlines Slammed by Mental Health Charities As "Simplistic"', in *The Huffington Post*, 27 March 2015.

Available at http://www.huffingtonpost.co.uk/2015/03/27/andreas-lubitz-depression-media-coverage-daily-mail-the-sun_n_6954666.html [Accessed 3rd April 2015].

Rodríguez, Clemencia, 2001, *Fissures in the Mediascape: An International Study of Citizen's Media*. Creskill, NJ: Hampton Press.

Rodríguez, Clemencia, Kidd, Dorothy and Stein, Laura (eds), 2010, *Creating New Communication Spaces*. Volume I of 'Making Our Media: Global Initiatives Toward a Democratic Public Sphere'. Cresskill, NJ: Euricom Monographs, Hampton Press.

Rose-Greenland, Fiona and Müge Göçek, Fatma, 2014 'Cultural Heritage and Violence in the Middle East', in OpenDemocracy. Available at https://www.opendemocracy.net/arab-awakening/fiona-rosegreenland-fatma-m%C3%BCge-g%C3%B6%C3%A7ek/cultural-heritage-and-violence-in-middle-east [Accessed April 2015].

Russo, A., 2012, 'The Rise of the "Media Museum": Creating Interactive Cultural Experiences Through Social Media', in Giaccardi, Elisa, (ed.), *Heritage and Social Media*. London and New York: Routledge, pp. 145–157.

Said, Edward, 1978/2003, *Orientalism: Western Conceptions of the Orient*. London: Penguin

Sandoval, Marisol and Fuchs, Christian, 2010, 'Towards a Critical Theory of Alternative Media', in *Telematics and Informatics*, 27(2):141–150.

Saunders, Nicholas, 2002, *The Poppy: A Cultural History from Ancient Egypt to Flanders Fields to Afghanistan*. London: One World Publications.

Saur, De Gruyter, 2011, *Museums of the World*. Germany: De Gruyter.

Saussure, Ferdinand de, 1959, *Course in General Linguistics*. New York: Philosophical Library.

Saville-Troike, Muriel, 1985, 'The Place of Silence in an Integrated Theory of Communication', in Tannen, Deborah and Saville-Troike, Muriel (eds), *Perspectives on Silence*. New Jersey: Ablex Publishing Corporation, pp. 3–19.

Schau, Hope Jensen and Gilly, Mary C., 2003, 'We Are What We Post? Self-Presentation in Personal Web Space', in *Journal of Consumer Research*, 30(3): 385–404.

Segaran, Toby and Hamerbacher, Jeff, 2009, *Beautiful Data: The Stories Behind Elegant Data Solutions*. CA: O'Reilly Media.

Sennett, Richard, 2008, *The Craftsman*. New Haven: Yale University Press.

Shifman, Limor, 2014, *Memes in Digital Culture*. Cambridge, MA and London: MIT Press.

Skeggs, Beverley, 2004, *Class, Self, Culture*. London and New York: Routledge.

Stabile, Carol, 2006, *White Victims, Black Villains: Gender, Race and Crime News in US Culture*. New York and Oxon: Routledge.

Stafford, Zach, 2015, 'If Transwomen Have to Hide to be Safe, What Does Progress Look Like?' in *The Guardian*, 6 March 2015. Available at http://www.theguardian.com/commentisfree/2015/mar/06/trans-women-hide-to-be-safe-what-progress-look-like?CMP=edit_2221 [Accessed 12th April 2015].

Stephens, Rebecca L., 2004, 'Socially Soothing Stories? Gender, Race and Class in TLC's A Wedding Story and A Baby Story', in Holmes, Su and Jermyn,

Deborah (eds), *Understanding Reality Television*. London and New York: Routledge, pp. 191–210.

Steyn, Juliet, 2014, 'Vicissitudes of Representation: Remembering and Forgetting', in Kidd, Jenny, Cairns, Sam, Drago, Alex, Ryall, Amy and Stearn, Miranda (eds), 2014, *Challenging History in the Museum: International Perspectives*. Surrey: Ashgate, pp. 141–148.

Storey, John, 2009, *Cultural Theory and Popular Culture* (5th Edition). Essex: Pearson Education.

Storey, John, 2012, *Cultural Theory and Popular Culture: An Introduction* (6th Edition). Essex: Pearson.

Tannen, Deborah and Saville-Troike, Muriel (eds), 1985, *Perspectives on Silence*. New Jersey: Ablex Publishing Corporation.

Tannen, Deborah, and Trester, Anna (eds), 2013, *Discourse 2.0: Language and New Media*. Washington, DC: Georgetown University Press.

Taylor, Astra, 2014, *The People's Platform: Taking Back Power and Culture in the Digital Age*. London: 4th Estate.

Telegraph, 2010, 'Student Tuition Fees Protests: Nick Clegg Says He Regrets Pre-election Pledge not to Increase Fees'. Available at http://www.telegraph.co.uk/education/universityeducation/8127315/Student-tuition-fees-protests-Nick-Clegg-says-he-regrets-signing-pre-election-pledge-not-to-increase-fees.html, 11th November 2010 [Accessed 6th April 2015].

Thompson, Alex, Stringfellow, Lindsay, Maclean, Mairi, MacLaren, Andrew, and O'Gorman, Kevin, 2014, 'Puppets of Necessity? Celebritisation in Structured Reality Television', in *Journal of Marketing Management*, 31(5–6): 478–501.

Thumim, Nancy, 2012, *Self-Representation and Digital Culture*. Hampshire and New York: Palgrave Macmillan.

TIME, 2013, Front Cover, 11th March edition. Available at http://time.com/3318830/pistorius [Accessed 8th July 2015].

Trans Media Watch, 2011, *The British Press and the Transgender Community: Submission to the Leveson Inquiry into the Culture, Practice and Ethics of the Press*. London: Trans Media Watch.

Trottier, Daniel, 2012, *Social Media as Surveillance: Rethinking Visibility in a Converging World*. Surrey: Ashgate.

Trottier, Daniel, 2014. *Identity Problems in the Facebook Era*. New York and London: Routledge.

Tumblr, 2015, 'Cumulative Total of Tumblr Blogs 2011–2015'. Available at http://www.statista.com/statistics/256235/total-cumulative-number-of-tumblr-blogs [Accessed February 2015].

Turkle, Sherry, 2011, *Alone Together: Why We Expect More from Technology and Less from Each Other*. New York: Basic Books.

Turkle, Sherry, 1995 (1997), *Life on the Screen: Identity in the Age of the Internet*. New York: Touchstone.

Turkle, Sherry, 1984, *The Second Self: Computers and the Human Spirit*. New York: Touchstone.

Tyler, Imogen and Bennett, Bruce, 2010, '"Celebrity Chav": Fame, Femininity and Social Class', in *European Journal of Cultural Studies*, 13(3): 375–393.

UNESCO, 2013, 'UN Broadband Commission Releases Latest Country-by-country Data on State of Broadband Access Worldwide', 21st September 2013. Available at http://www.unesco.org/new/en/media-services/single-view/news/un_broadband_commission_releases_latest_country_by_country_data_on_state_of_broadband_access_worldwide/#.VVSC6WZuoWo [Accessed 13th May 2015].

U.S. Army, undated, 'About America's Army: The Official U.S. Army Game', on Facebook page, https://www.facebook.com/americasarmygame/info?tab=page_info [Accessed 27th April 2015].

Van Dijck, Jose, 2013, '"You Have One Identity": Performing the Self on Facebook and LinkedIn', in *Media, Culture and Society*, 35(2): 199–215.

Vanmetre, Elizabeth, 2015, 'Jamie Foxx Blasted on Twitter for Joke about Bruce Jenner's Transition during iHeartRadio Awards'. Available at http://www.nydailynews.com/entertainment/tv/jamie-foxx-blasted-comments-made-bruce-jenner-article-1.2166546 [Accessed 1st April 2015].

Walkowitz, Daniel J. and Knauer, Lisa Maya, 2009, *Contested Histories in Public Space: Memory, Race and Nation*. Durham, NC: Duke University Press.

Webb, Jen, 2009, *Understanding Representation*. LA, London, New Delhi, Singapore, Washington, DC: SAGE.

Weedon, Chris, 2004, *Identity and Culture: Narratives of Difference and Belonging*. Berkshire: Open University Press.

Weltman, David, 2008, 'Popular Representations of the Working Class: Contested Identities and Social Change', paper available at http://www.beyondcurrenthorizons.org.uk/popular-representations-of-the-working-class-contested-identities-and-social-change [Accessed 10th May 2015].

Wesch, Michael, 2009, 'YouTube and You: Experiences of Self-awareness in the Context Collapse of the Recording Webcam', in *Explorations in Media Ecology*, 8(2): 19–34.

Wettergren, Åsa, 2009, 'Fun and Laughter: Culture Jamming and the Emotional Regime of Late Capitalism', in *Social Movement Studies*, 8(1): 1–10.

White, Michael, 2010, 'David Cameron Should Not Have Worn that Poppy in China', *The Guardian*, Wednesday, 10th November 2010. Available at http://www.theguardian.com/politics/blog/2010/nov/10/david-cameron-poppy-china-michael-white [Accessed 27th January 2015].

Williams, R., 2012 http://www.independent.co.uk/life-style/gadgets-and-tech/news/revealed-the-third-largest-country-in-the-world--facebook-hits-one-billion-users-8197597.html [Accessed 13th April 2015].

Wintour, Patrick, 2012, 'Nick Clegg Apologises for Tuition Fees Pledge', in *The Guardian*, Thursday, 20th September. Available at http://www.theguardian.com/politics/2012/sep/19/nick-clegg-apologies-tuition-fees-pledge [Accessed 6th April 2015].

Wodak, Ruth and Meyer, Michael, 2009, *Methods for Critical Discourse Analysis* (2nd Edition). London, CA, New Delhi and Singapore: SAGE.

Wood, Helen and Skeggs, Beverley, 2011, *Reality Television and Class*. London: Palgrave Macmillan.

Woods, Faye, 2012, 'Classed Femininity, Performativity, and Camp in British Structured Reality Programming', in *Television and New Media*, 20(10): 1–18.

Wordpress, 2015, 'A Live Look at Activity across WordPress.com'. Available at https://en.wordpress.com/activity/?v=6&source=googleUKWebblog&campaign=hsb&currency=pound&type=&term=Wordpress%20blog&gclid=CjwKEAiAg_CnBRDc1N_wuoCiwyESJABpBuMXlqzNzeO_XYwFMVwAS5paBWdsq6Mtcp1oBfjEoHFqVRoCxMTw_wcB [Accessed February 2015].

Yandoli, Krystie Lee, 2015, 'Comedians Under Fire for Transphobic Bruce Jenner Jokes at The Justin Bieber Roast', 31st March 2015. Available at http://www.buzzfeed.com/krystieyandoli/bruce-jenner-was-the-butt-of-all-the-jokes-at-the-justin-bie#.ok94KVNYR [Accessed 1st April 2015].

YouTube, 2015, 'Statistics'. Available at https://www.youtube.com/yt/press/en-GB/statistics.html [Accessed March 2015].

Zappavigna, Michele, 2012, *Discourse of Twitter and Social Media: How We Use Language to Create Affiliation on the Web*. London and New York: Continuum Books.

Zappavigna, Michele, 2011, 'Ambient Affiliation: A Linguistic Perspective on Twitter', in *New Media and Society*, 13(5): 788–806.

Zara, Christopher, 2012, 'Is Twitter Making Us Meaner? Uncivil Discourse in the Age of Social Media', in *International Business Times*, 1st December 2012. Available at http://www.ibtimes.com/twitter-making-us-meaner-uncivil-discourse-age-social-media-909856 [Accessed March 2015].

INDEX

Note: page numbers in *italics* denotes an illustration